CRAZY

MELON

and

CHINESE

APPLE

CRAZY MELON
and
CHINESE APPLE

The Poems of
Frances Chung

Compiled and with an Afterword by Walter K. Lew

Wesleyan University Press
Published by University Press of New England
Hanover and London

Wesleyan University Press

Published by University Press of New England, Hanover, NH 03755

Printed in the United States of America

5   4   3   2   1

Text design by C. Y. Design.

Library of Congress Cataloging-in-Publication Data
Chung, Frances, 1950–1990.
    Crazy melon and Chinese apple : the poems of Frances Chung / compiled, and with an afterword by Walter K. Lew.
        p.   cm.
Includes index.
    ISBN 0–8195–6415–x (alk. paper)—ISBN 0–8195–6416–8 (pbk. : alk. paper)
    1. Chinatown (New York, N.Y.)—Poetry. 2. Lower East Side (New York, N.Y.)—Poetry. 3. Chinese Americans—Poetry. I. Lew, Walter K. II. Title.
PS3553.H7935 C73   2000
811'.54—dc21   00–009337

CONTENTS

CRAZY MELON

CHINESE APPLE

OTHER POEMS

COMMENTARY

CRAZY MELON

For the Chinatown people

Yo vivo en el barrio chino
de Nueva York . . . I live in
New York's Chinatown. Some
call it a ghetto, some call
it a slum, some call it home.
Little Italy or Northern
Chinatown, to my mind, the
boundaries have become fluid.
I have two Chinatown moods.
Times when Chinatown is a
terrible place to live in.
Times when Chinatown is the
only place to live . . .

The echoes of the night trucks
bouncing off the cobblestones
on Canal Street play on the
silences in my bones. Playing
games with the red and green
light on the corner of Mott and
Canal, we find an excuse to run—
we who know that those who are
brave cross Mott Street on a
diagonal.

References to your home as a ghetto. Ancient
tenements. Sociological labels. A Chinese
wonderland.

No one uses words such as
marvelous here. The scent
of incense trails through
the hallway in the early
morning. Buddhist altars
are erected loosely on
kitchen tables. The ashes
of the incense gather dust
as do the faded photographs
of families in China and the
calendars of nude redheads
on the wall. Listen to the
78 rpm Chinese records.

welcome to Chinatown ladies and gentlemen
the place where you tourists come to look
at the slanted eyes yellow skin scaling fish
roast duck in the windows like a public hanging
ooh the pitter patter of the slippers
oh look the cute Chinese children with their schoolbags
hurry grab your camera to take a picture
next to a pagoda telephone booth
to show your grandchildren what you know
does anyone know the number
who owns the list of dreams wives and families
left behind somewhere far across an ocean
see what you can behind the dragon lights
the taut faces that mask thought and feeling
(the bus leaves for the Statue of Liberty at two)
Chinatown is a place to go eat chinks
where happiness has resigned itself
to have tea every Sunday afternoon

One black boy on a class trip
points to a glass figurine of
an arhat in the windowcase of
a souvenir shop and shouts
excitedly: Hey, look at that
ninety year man!

Neon lights that warm no one. How long
ago have we stopped reading the words
and the colors? On Saturday night,
the streets are so crowded with people
that to walk freely I have to walk in
the gutter. The visitors do not hear
you when you say excuse me. They are
so busy taking in the wonders of Chinatown.
People line up to enter the restaurant
(you must know which one). The way
the couples hold each other they make
it seem like Coney Island. They are
busy looking for Buddhas and gifts to
take home. Some men are looking for
'Asian chicks.' There is a deficiency
of Chinese couples. Windchimes chime on.
Bells ring on. Paperweights sit and
stare as if from under a pond. The
irony reeks.

The movie theater filled with sticky
soda gum wrappers and the smell of
cigarette smoke and take-out orders
from the restaurants. The restrooms
are haunted by ghosts that smell of
urine. Chinese babies crying. No
seats. Woman getting out of her seat
to walk her baby in the back of the
theater. Her husband is sitting four
rows behind her. Cartons of Chinese
food, crackling of peanut shells and
all that beautiful sword action on
the screen mirroring the inner strength
and fantasy of a few in the audience
who see themselves living as presentday
warriors, swordswomen, emperors or
concubines. Blood running like thin
acrylic ketchup. Revenge honor filial
piety and the flow of chi. Chinese
men on their day off. Young people
skipping school. A sprinkle of black
and Puerto Rican karate students.
Women whose husbands are working late.
After the midnight show (this is not
the Apollo) the single men out on the
streets in a group scattered by the
wind on Chatham Square to their
apartments as eyes focus on a slightly
different world.

Philodendron plants. Monk's food and
noodles. Holy water. Orange and white
jewels and light create an aura around
the figure of Kuan Yin. The Buddhist
temple changes its location. The image
of the idols and soul tablets being
moved along Canal Street fascinates me.

They dress alike and cut their black hair into shag cuts. They wear the same high heels. Some of the girls dye their hair red. Some of the boys get a permanent. They speak Chinese sprinkled with many English words.

They are seen in different
parts of town scanning windows
for something of interest to
pass the evening time. Unmarried
or married it is hard to tell
when these Chinese men wear no
wedding rings and show no sign
of being in or out of love. I
saw a man waiting for a bus
tonight. Womanless.

The hare krishna people come
to Chinatown chanting om om om
beating their drums and carrying
their babies. The Chinese
people avoid them and stare at
their shaven heads. They look
like pale white ghosts.

Walking along the Bowery, can't
help but think of the saddest
place in the world, the street
of blind prostitutes in Hong Kong.

bread

come walk the streets of the bowery where time is not
and hear hard luck tales of gypsy men
whimper with the man whose wife left him
and took their three children
with the man who wanted to be a writer poet something
with the phd man who needed a decade
to learn that knowledge rots
with the man making his third comeback
touch frostbitten hands faces lips
mumbling their stories to someone absenced
with roof of old gray hats
the gypsy men with pocket full of holes
count their slippery fistful of coins
five six times to pass the time
living day to day by the grace of god
walking nowhere seeing no one thing
but eliot images of youth forsaken in bar mirrors
watching boxing matches on glary black and white screen
deus ex machina
timidly hold back as your brother treasure hunts
amid stinking garbage cans runneth over
take a handle as he drags along
shopping bag of clinking hollow bottles
look into his bleeding eyes when
he comes to your car window
with his spit and t-shirt rag
huddle with the gypsy men sprawled over
the streets of the bowery
bundles of raggedy andy dolls
and tell me you care

bread #2

black voices hit the air
men shooting red craps
surprise pee
falling in a fountain
impeach nixon banner
jazz flute flying from
archie shepp's fire escape
a prostitute's window

surrealists on east houston

a brick wall is painted in layers of piss and smells
the surrealists paint signs that read
virgo & virgo 4 ever (in a heartshaped frame)
pussy is ice cream
S. B. 110
a tough young woman in a gypsy scarf paints her lips red
one surrealist's name is Blue
and wears a pin in the form of a palette
the surrealists dream of red sneakers

There are more Chinese bums
in the neighborhood now. No
one knows where they come from
but they appear with crazy
smiles and unshaven faces.
One of them looks like a poet.

Aside from the trees in Columbus Park
and the tree along Canal Street that I
call my tree because it mirrors my
inner seasons, there are no green forests
in sight. Bamboo is eaten out of a
can and appears in the names applied to
the people, depending on which side of
the ocean you were born. The gingko tree
is a restaurant where my father and
brothers serve well-to-do white people
gourmet clichés of sweet and sour pork,
eggrolls, and spareribs. We are
forgetting the fan-shaped leaves of wind
and ripple.

it is the same walk
past the tired streets
following the dust trails
the garbage still overflowing
bags of potato chips still being bought
rings of children that push and leave
who don't know the meaning of goodbye
for whom did you think it would change color?

oh lucky me
I am of some use
I am of some inspiration
to the two men
across the lunchcounter
I remind them of the
last Chinese restaurant
they took their family to
did you know that
Chinese food was delicious?

On New Year's Eve we throw the
I Ching. I receive the hexagram:
the power of the great.

Chinese New Year. Yellow chrysanthemums
on the middle of the kitchen table make
everyone smile inside and out. The
festive octagon of candy and nuts is
waiting for the hands of children and
visitors. Isolated firecrackers.
Firecrackers blazing from parking meters.
Old men hats. Baby smiles. Banners
across Chinatown. So many dragons to
follow. Oranges to cut. Shrimp chips
flowering.

the winter wind sits in the living room
so we huddle in the kitchen
in our winter coats looking silly
and too cold to do anything
but light a candle eat melon seeds
as I wonder
what do we wear when we go outside?

a flower lifts on Mott Street
through window pane and
oily morning
a flower turns to color
the sky with pastel softness
to touch the stones on the
streets that bruised
the knees of the children
the flower that defies
sanitation trucks
motorcycle noise
out of order telephone booths
and oven laundromats
that sings a fresh song
every dawning

The summer nights we spent on the cool stoops. We wore our keys around our necks. Summer breezes produced by the spray of the fire hydrants. Rivers in the gutters, floating garbage to the sewers. Watching the colored papers drift by—paper cups, gum wrappers suddenly turned into boats of fortune. Children in the neighborhood took off their shoes and socks and went wading. The summer when Japanese rubber sandals made their appearance and replaced sneakers. We couldn't have them because they were too expensive. Italian ices were dreams of tutti-frutti and chocolate dribbled onto blouses. Edna, being the oldest, had to go home first to prepare the bathtub. It was in the kitchen with a heavy, white lid. All the food jars, cereal boxes, and cans on the lid had to be removed, the roaches killed. Sometimes the lid was just balanced between two chairs and it turned into a bazaar of miscellaneous goodies.

We stole a snail from the outdoor baskets in front of the Italian grocery store and took it home in our pockets. Once there, we placed it gingerly on the kitchen table and waited for it to make its appearance, spraying drops of water from our fingers to see if it was home.

Goofy Lala was the wicked woman who lived on Elizabeth Street who caught children and put them in her basement. It was taboo to say her name out loud. She could be seen during feast times, mingling with the crowd. We teased Louisa the Bum because she wore no panties and then ran away quickly because she threw bottles when she became angry.

We spent summer afternoons catching flies that hovered over the garbage cans and walls of the seafood restaurant on the corner. Catching the small black insects, releasing them from the palms of our hands—it was a game with us— the funny feel of the fly fluttering around in our closed palms. Mother said the flies were dirty because they sat on dog shit. There were times when a giant insect flew into the neighborhood. An outsider, truly a stranger. And no butterflies. At night, we were back at the restaurant, peering through the window at rich funny people eating spaghetti. Only now do I realize what the pink neon sign read—wines.

My Italian girlfriends dressed up on Sundays in dresses and heels. They told me they were going to eat chinks after confession. I thought that this was either someone's house or the name of a restaurant. Little did I know they were headed for Chinatown. Not having any spending money, and never going to church, I never joined them. We went our separate ways on Sundays.

On Saturday, it is 14th Street for shopping. Clothes at a bargain. The women who work in the clothing factories find the clothes that they sew in the department stores selling at a much higher price than what they received for their labor. For a treat, you can have lunch at Nedicks or pizza at the five-and-ten. The earring peddler on the street will see that you don't want to buy from him and will tell you to go back to Chinatown only you really don't know this happened because you don't understand English. Little do you know that this same man will tell the same thing to your daughter on an uptown street.

Every Sunday, we go to 'Jew Street,' Orchard Town, to shop for bargains. We go into the fabric stores with their printed fabrics, gardens of flowers. The prickly smell of textile and old air in the narrow shops make the eyes smart. The Chinese women complain by waving a hand in the stuffy air and placing a hand over mouth and nose. The Jewish owners sometimes get angry if you linger too long without buying anything and will tell you to leave the store. If you are nice enough, one may offer you a bite of his cheese danish. The Chinese children, part-time translators and usually daughters, wait outside sitting on the stoops or else eagerly select material for a new dress. A few yards of fabric will go a long way this slow, sunny Sunday.

Walking through the streets for hours like this, gradually accumulating bags of food, clothing, treasures of the day. Pickles in barrels, chandeliers, pizza, mountains of shoes.

Walking among the black, Puerto Rican and white people. Watching out for pickpockets and dirty men. Window shopping becomes a dream. The underwear stores are boring. Our young eyes never quite believing the miniature sofas we saw in the drapery shops.

An excursion into the Essex Street market where you will be blessed for buying figs. It could be Mexico or Peru. Pike fish, banana soda, patatas, platanos, religious candles and occult books written in Spanish.

Running along the bridal shops on Grand Street, rediscovered in the diaries of Anais Nin, choosing your 'bride,' who you would be in a crazy mixed up fairy tale, before your sisters beat you to it. Flower girls receiving special priority because they were young like you and if you stood on tiptoe maybe you could look straight into their blue mannequin eyes. Some brides stood proudly without heads, one-armed, even one naked bride with no nipples.

Mango did not know what she wanted. Not from the bleached walls of the city buildings, the dots of soot on the windowsills, nor even the curiously designed paper clips in the aluminum offices with their typewriter rhythms and hum. She tried touching them to see, as though that one easy movement would solve the mysteries in her mind. Listening raptly for any possible message she might learn from the bells of the doors and churches, she kept with her the peculiar air of each place she would walk through or by.

Things belonging to Mango grew in clusters like bunches of soap bubbles that swelled, and burst just as quickly, with each encounter with a new friend or stranger. Her possessions were too fragile. One by one, like drops of alcohol from winter icicles, her people and memories failed her. At times she felt as if she was losing her dimple; the hole so deeply a part of her was filling up with sand from the littered boardwalks of her past.

She feared old age, of losing her beauty visible only occasionally in sun and shadow of mirrors. She wondered why she was saving her soft clothes, dreambook, and Rilke jewels and streets for the dim idea drowning like a dying fire in the black centers of her eyes. But she continued to do so, as she continued to do many things.

In the midst of a talk with a friend, she would suddenly find the insides of her cheeks feeling as if they wanted to cry out, with tears like the particles of air in a taut balloon, begging freedom and room. She felt like dropping so many things into a well—they and some parts of her were so useless. At other moments, she would think she would never be as happy again. Times when she would be running on the wind or listening to children talking.

35

And yet, she was always afraid that she was missing out on something. Afraid that she had forgotten to do something important. Afraid that she would lose her power to dream.

(Western Electric)

Please don't tell me you're sorry. Don't bother. That flower you're holding sheepishly in your hand looks like it passed away during the Middle Ages. I struck my last match many nights and lifetimes ago. I had never noticed the loneliness carried in an empty matchbook. I burned my fingers looking for the candles and no one was here to share the hurt as I cried out to empty space. Like a maniac (I couldn't see my reflection in the mirror), I tried frantically to bar the uninvited entrance of light. But painful and blinding, the day came to intrude on my dimmest thoughts. Like a cruel prison guard, it laughingly shined its searchlight on the maps on the ceiling, the bumps in the wallpaper, the dusty linoleum, and the paths in my palms. Finally, it chanced fatefully upon the books of our prophets sprawled suddenly disgustingly over the stove and telephone stand. One by one.

A casual observer, a lady walking her dog, or the mailman, would have remarked that the light that morning was a gray gentle mist from the harbor, but to me it was the fiercest white I had seen for the longest while. The tangerine peels, gatekeepers to the doors of incense, and cryptic symbol of the Chinese garden we had in a dream, whimpered and died. I mourn for them and the dreadful memories that will possess me after you silently close the door, leaving your shadow standing on the wall.

in a corner of the subway door discovered
one squashed chocolate football
the silent memories of the pigeons
and you in every tree

mosquito
singing
there'll be no
love song
tonight

they must have me learn my lessons of violence
these experiences hells
in these hallways of 'duck shit' green
they come out to teach me from the dark
cursing to myself (shi-i-t) in a word that crosses
the length of my body
as the Chinese man asks me a question one day
only to come after me the next
with his quiet thing on a quiet Sunday
the white guy on the corner in the snow
follows me up the stairs
in his silent rubber boots two steps at a time
the girls on the block throw bubble gum
push and threaten in race games of jealousy
they in their high heels
they don't know
they don't care
who I am
what I've been through
that I've seen enough of this shit
and there are bars silent words on the walls
neighbors minding their business
watching dumb television shows
dogs barking at the wrong time
signs warning against rats
janitors declaring
no more pepperoni in the toilet bowls

It would have been nice if people saw her as she saw herself, but things were never so 'nice.' Living in a neighborhood where her dark haired beauty brought only furtive looks from the sanitation men in the morning and the tired Chinese men coming home from work at night on the subway, she wished that people could just smile, say hello without wanting anything more. The freedom to walk the streets at night without being thought a naughty girl, without the fear of being raped. When she looked around her to see who else was on the quiet streets, it seemed that the one or two people out were running home.

There was that soft-spoken young man from New England who had called her a 'delicate flower' and asked whether she was Japanese. But he thought of her as a rose and she saw herself as a chrysanthemum.

There were the Puerto Rican men who called her a 'sweet Jap' or more often, 'chinita.' And she wanted to reply 'Véte al carajo.' The Greek men in the souvlaki restaurants calling out to her in their accents 'Susie Wong.' Then she remembered that when she was younger the men in the neighborhood said the same thing to her friend's mother, who was called 'Susie,' although this was not her name at all. The young man stopping her in the street to say 'Arigato' and then looking hurt when she explained that she was not Japanese. And then the old man who whispered as she walked past on Mott Street 'Do you ever play with yourself? You and me . . . I could really sock it to you.'

Friends wrote from Europe wishing her a Happy Valentine's Day.

Piropos de la chinita

mamita linda
muñeca
chiquitita
mommy
corazón de melón

the magician growing bean sprouts
making baby soft breaking beancurd
listening to the tinkle of sugar
in chrysanthemum tea
we tasted the roast pork buns
looking for the right one

they want me to settle down
when I have not yet lived
mother talking to me in songs
of shopping bags and movie star calendars
given for free at the grocery store
(she wants a grandson)
with hopes of mooncakes dragon bracelets
and ginger soup
they want me to settle down
with the nice young man from Brooklyn
with the car and college degree
but every cockroach that runs across
my mind
whispers that I haven't seen Peking

There is a group of Chinese-American men who think of themselves as Chinese warriors. They are beautiful anachronisms. They study the martial arts, practice calligraphy, consult the I Ching and go to sword flicks to blow their minds.

this Chinese warrior
breaks the teabowl
with his chi
he knows all around him
without looking
every step is clear
in the right direction
with power flowing
from the middle of his palm
he can move mountains
he never looks back
and tells no one his name

that Zen time in the snow
with sound of meditation bell
a long black robe
flowing in the wind
strength of mind
clearness of head
quaker bread
retreat into New England
no snowballs here
everything is pleasant

dream collection
a man with dashiki lips
two peaches beneath a tree

Discovery of the secret power to
dream in Chinese. Chinese characters
dangle before my eyes on a black
wired mobile. I don't think I
can read them.

The cockroach dream nightmare. Banging
on the kitchen table a funky jazz beat.
Me the drummer banging so hard the steel
rim of the table flew off. Under the
table a huge family of cockroaches.
They started running off in seven
different directions. Me too running
off in seven different directions.
One cockroach image remained—one
overturned on its back struggling. I
must reread *Metamorphosis*.

behind the chatter
a transparent clear
pink glass egg
the color of seashells
if you look into it
you can have the ocean

We use newspaper for a
tablecloth. And when I
want to make my mother
sad I tell her that I'm
going to cook American
food when I am older.

Where is the cockroach who left
its footprint on my bowl?

Don't leave any rice in your
bowl, or your future husband
will have pockmarks in his face.
One mark to match every piece
of rice you don't eat.
(A childlike memory of washing
rice and measuring the water
needed to cook the rice with
index finger.)

When the water in the pot is about to boil, when the bubbles have appeared and are beginning to move around, we say that the water is singing a song.

If it is true that you are what you
eat then I am many souls, many flavors
and essences. Ginger root, salty balls,
beancurd, salted fish, mushrooms of
immortality, winter melon, western
melon . . . Drinking tea is drinking
nature itself. Leaves, twigs and the
discovery of a field of chrysanthemums
in a teapot.

I am fruit crazy. I love six
persimmons, Pablo Neruda lemons,
dragon eyes, lichee nuts (pits to
be carved into a tiny bucket),
yellow bananas, mangos, oranges
(Chinese New Year oranges, the
original 'china'), tangerines,
mandarins and Chinese apples.
Here, pomegranates (granadas) are
called Chinese apples. It is a joy
to discover the insides of one.
An incredibly beautiful red.
Hundreds of jewels hiding beneath
translucent skin. Spanish fruits
are feminine.

Fruit Mutations

grape approaching lichee
peach approaching mango

(Europe)

I have very little
to call mine
but every day
I weave my hair
into a straight braid
my clothes have
but a few shapes
and colors
they do not feel soft
like any part of me
but my hair
after all these days
is still soft and black
it grows and obeys me

do you remember when it seemed the whole world
was closed
on shrimp gray days
the rain held us in
we saw Lincoln Center from a bus
elegance was a Greek restaurant
the New York Times was too big to fold
with too many dictionary words empty crosswords
they never reported the killing
down the street
the clothes they advertised were unreal too
who lounged who wore bathrobes
who had a dining room
everything in life being guesswork
cooking without teaspoons
eternal windowshoppers
we women were sometimes like children

Lunchtime at the factory is a family affair. Mother and three daughters. The daughters disappear periodically to go to school. One is 13 years old. Husband and wife running the show. The noise stops for a brief respite but the sewing activity really doesn't. Preparations for the afternoon hours. Folding collars and pockets. Knowing both sides of cloth. Tying manufacturer's labels that you can't read yourself. You have your own identification number. Getting your share of the free tea before the supply is exhausted. Going to the bathroom of no toilet paper. Punching out. Taking out lunch cooked in the morning or food from last night's dinner in thermos or baby food jars. The Chinese jars that one can recognize by shape. Rice for sustenance. Food from Chinatown and its sweet creamy coffee. The latest Glamour styles are sewn for a few pennies. Doesn't the dust get into your lungs? What kind of lunch hour is this? Thirty minutes.

Chewing rhythms. Playing with the black cat with the collar. Rice bundles and hard boiled eggs. The loudspeaker plays Chinese music to make you think that you are in a Chinese movie, at home, or relaxing in Canton. Overtime is natural. And the talk. Are goldfish eyes hereditary then? Husbands. This one cooks dinner for me. My stupid one left me because I didn't give him children. What I make each day is not enough to buy a chicken.

When the sewing is good (prices are high) at the factory, the women are happy. They say that they are eating 'soy sauce chicken.' One woman says that she takes the number 11 bus to work, meaning her two legs.

The factory ladies, grateful for elevators and drafts of fresh air, develop a bent back from their positions at work.

They sometimes wear cloth masks over their mouths, like doctors in an operating room. (No one has heard of D. H. Lawrence.)

The threads in your machine are entangled. You have made a mistake and must take apart your sewing. Beyond the fire escape you can see into other factories, through replicas of your own dust-ridden window. Lunchtime is suddenly over.

I discover the other women in my family. My
grandmother on Mulberry Street is the buttonhole
lady in her factory. She earns a penny for each
buttonhole she makes and does not complain. She
is a collector of buttons and material scraps.
I have lunch with her at Woolworth's and am amazed
at her spirit and appetite. My grandmother in
Hong Kong buys the coconut candy she loves. Living
with a daughter-in-law who neglects her, giving
birth to more than a dozen children, never earning
a cent in her life, combing her long hair in the
early morning when she cannot sleep. One lone
image of my mother having dinner Saturday night at
Kentucky Fried Chicken after a day's hard work.
Conversation with my mother is restricted. Any
talk about love, art, books, films, sex is out of
the question. Marriage is a topic to be avoided
since it leads to arguments and discontent. I am
limited to sentences like, "I've just eaten half
an orange at grandma's."

Sitting across from me on the bus a Chinese couple and their young son. The wife is not accustomed to riding in automobiles so she feels nauseous and uncomfortable. She cups her hand over her mouth as if to vomit. Finally, she opens her pocketbook to fish out pieces of coconut candy, offering one to her husband and son wordlessly. They are headed for Chinatown with shopping bags of groceries. They do not speak much to each other and when they do, they speak a different dialect. The scene is reenacted endless times with the stage sometimes shifting to the subway.

Riding the subway is an adventure
especially if you cannot read the signs.
One gets lost. One becomes anxious and
does not know whether to get off when
the other Chinese person in your car
does. (Your crazy logic tells you that
the both of you must be headed for the
same stop.) One woman has discovered the
secret of one-to-one correspondence.
She keeps the right amount of pennies
in one pocket and upon arriving in each
new station along the way she shifts one
penny to her other pocket. When all the
pennies in the first pocket have disappeared,
she knows that she is home.

he was growing old
without a wife
so he worked for
ten years sweating
in an oily kitchen
so he could buy one
with promises of a
new country where
sat a gold mountain
richer than the sun
so the dream arrived in
his one room place
was frightened by the
black people and the
cold weather but
decided to try and
enlisted in the factory
squad the next day
only to find that
she wanted more

I call her the tea lady (to myself) because I only see her taking care of the teacups in the association. She seems imported.

He wears a uniform of red and black
flannel shirt adding a brown vest
and Chinese jacket with silk wadding
in the wintertime. He has an old
brown leather jacket with a fur collar
as wrinkled as his skin that any artist
in the village would be proud to wear.
For a refrigerator, he has placed two
wooden crates outside the window.
Living with his door unlocked, he has
been collecting Quaker Oats boxes for
twenty years now. They are empty and
full of dust.

Beekman Downtown

the elevator smells of an operation
a pregnancy or open heart surgery
plastic trays roll in and out
they are part of the routine
of days framed by Venetian blinds
(the sun may not show today)
smiling nurses offer oranges
it is Chinese New Year
there are signs in Chinese
but no one speaks the language
in this hotel for transients
flowers begin to die
the moment they enter the door

He came down the hall with blackness in his pupils, sick with thinness, sober on alcohol. "Glad to see you, come into the visitors' room where there is more heat." This is spoken slowly, with effort, in Chinese. Head wobbly like the rest of his frame broken with liver. How do you say 'cirrhosis of the liver' in Chinese? We had four pink carnations for him, but he didn't want to impose on the orderlies for a vase as he didn't want to ask for a blanket although he was cold. No blanket could warm the winter in his bones. Blankets he described as mosquito netting, burlap for beggars. He may be poor, but he was no beggar. His pride was too strong. No notion of the time of day, but he made himself a calendar. He was used to living in a world where sight was limited. He could not read English, but he was curious enough to walk over to the Sunday Times on the table and point out for you the date '16.' Out of the multitude of life in the newsprint, he could pick out that number. Seventy-two years old and seventy dollars saved from a lifetime in America. A roll of crumpled bills hidden under the linoleum to be sent to his wife in China, by now, a forgotten face and body. He envies you because you have the gift of listening to the weather report on the radio. He can only look out the window and guess for himself. He will jump out of his hospital window. Before you leave, he will ask you to bring toothpicks the next time you come.

that stiff figure there
that man
in the box with maroon velvet sides
lips colored orange gummed silent
is not my grandfather
did not wave to me from a window
as I came home from school
did not make jello for me
did not bring me to the movies every Saturday
did not tease my grandmother
about her funny ways
did not smoke Chesterfields
did not walk with pendulum stride
swinging brown trouser legs
baggy
yet he has a mole on his left cheek
the wailing incense red candles
will not bring him back
and the tears they come

viet nam
bomb
have you seen my mother's
head
i am bleeding to death
what is he saying
the president of the
united states of america
i don't understand english
there are black clouds
in the air
my house is a black cloud
why is this man taking
my picture when
i don't know how to smile
any more
my life is at war with
itself
viet nam
bomb

Taiwan

the place where
sunrise and sunset
are still
points of time

small child holding
hand of small child
holding hand of small
child carrying
baby sleeping

we must not scratch
our names onto the bamboo
or the birds
will lose their way

a baby's cry
another mouth to feed

you are not my son
you have come home
without finishing
the day's work

I will come to
America one day
I will open a shop
where I will make
Chinese seals
labelled by nature and
circled by time

sun moon lake
where the echoes of
the aborigines remain
fixed to the trunks
in the forests and
imaginary snakes
find their way
to your sandals

stretches of green
broken only by
bright patches of
red and pink flowers
on the bundles that
the women carry
on their back

layers of skin and brownness
where the trucks
make a strange noise
a village is known by its smell
the dogs slow and thin
hands muscles sweat and bend
to make the melons grow

the tea leaves changed
as the days passed
islands became circles
became sun and
everything came true

Hong Kong

into the hallway
up the stairway without rail
my mother grew up
on dark steps like these
dust clay and smoked-out fire
with a dog put to sleep by the incense
buying medicine from a family having dinner
there are no women
the vegetables on the table smell of medicine
in the oilcovered room
the plants have stopped growing and are shrinking
like the faces of the old men
                              (Hollywood Street)

nightclub bathroom
dirty stink
old woman sitting inside
handing out towels
eating dinner at the same time
while we drop coins
into her plate

I went to sleep last night
thinking of Aberdeen with
its sea animals rocking chair boats
and shameless beggars
in my dreams I came
to the country of
Abalonia

I will bring you
to a pawnshop
one day

The young man dressed in white is a barber at
the airport. He teases you in Spanish. When
you answer him in Spanish he follows you down
the corridors of waiting rooms. His father
was Chinese and came from Hong Kong. His last
name is Jung. His mother is Mexican. When
his parents died seven years ago, he came to
this country to be a barber. He wants to learn
Chinese. He has a book in his shop for this
purpose, but the language is difficult to learn.
When he questions you, you lie to him and say
you have a husband. He looks disappointed,
smiles and walks away in the direction of the
men's room. You are on the way to Lima.

En busca del barrio chino de Lima . . .
Many centuries ago, the British came with their ships
loaded with Chinese people. They were traded as slaves
to the Peruvians in exchange for gold. The Chinese
brought with them their knowledge of rice and rice is
now eaten everyday in Peru. El barrio chino is larger
than that of San Francisco, Boston, Amsterdam or New York.
In the Chinatown, an arch is erected which seems to be in
the way of the vendors and people in the marketplace.
There are old lean Chinese men with young looks on their
faces. There is a beautiful mixture of races. Many
Peruvians have black hair and slanted eyes. The babies
have round faces. The Chinese intermarry with the Indians,
but the Japanese do not. Peruvian women, faces baked by
the sun like the hot food they are selling give milk from
their breast to babies, smiling and telling the baby to
drink. Chinese pastry shops, coffee shops, chicken
markets, imported Japanese photograph albums and rice
bowls. The few signs in Chinese are elementary and
simplified. The people speak Cantonese. When they
speak Spanish, they appear to be strangers. Chinese
restaurants called 'chifas.' Chinese vegetables, bean
sprouts, tamales wrapped in dark green leaves bound
with string. The Incan names—Chimu, Chancay,
Chan-Chan, Chunga . . . Chan Chung.

And if I said 'ming' to you
would you answer
would you hear me

[*Missing Poem*]

of three minds

forest selva　林

flower flor　花

moon luna　月

rain lluvia　雨

bamboo bambú　竹

scenes gathered from a Chinese-English dictionary:
clouds clearing away
simple clothing
rose flower cake
coral chopsticks
night shining pearl
to gaze at the ocean and sigh
third day after a child's birth
moon clouded over
to give rice to the poor
husband of a wife's younger sister
to lie down undressed and sigh constantly
lunar mansion
to hold the knees and sing away
throw an embroidered ball in choosing a husband
to drown infants
first woman who taught Chinese people how to make silk
    from silkworm
unknown hero born in the country
to enjoy chrysanthemums
fireflies at the window and snow on the table
with as many children as grasshoppers
anti-mosquito incense
incense sticks indicating time
double pillow used by newly married people
silence of three minutes
embroidered robes with axes drawn on them in black and
    white
beautiful girl from a lower family
bamboo chair for mountain traveler
small open basket for holding rice

the yellow carp
white jasmine
kneel while incense burns
fried dough strips
a Buddhist word
bound feet of woman
to play at Chinese chess
a Taoist priest's robe
worms in books, clothes, or wood
carry dish with hands
songs of stilt walkers
overfed baby vomits
coconut shell as ladle
to rub Chinese ink
whitish jade ear-plugs
a stroke to the right in writing
take off slipper
my dull mind is suddenly opened

Glossary

舊飯   *a piece of rice*—term applied to a lazy person, especially husbands; an idler, sitting there like 'a piece of rice.'

冷飯   *cold rice*—term applied to the rice left in the pot; left-over rice, placed in the refrigerator to be cooked tomorrow; principal ingredient of fried rice.

老豆   *old bean*—derogatory term applied to one's father; analogous to the English 'my old man.'

金魚眼   *goldfish eyes*—pop-eyes; self-explanatory term.

細蚊仔   *little mosquitoes*—children.

鴨屎綠   *duck shit green*—olive green.

CHINESE APPLE

For Li Po

they read your poem still
at the New School
in Pound's translation

at West Lake your spirit
mingles with Su Tung Po's
a willow path is named for you

in Shanghai we found you
reclining in a Friendship store
carved out of an olive pit

in Chinatown a waiter tells of
the time you visited Hangchow
was it there you took your life

you will be pleased to know
your legend lives on
we remember your middle name

eating oranges

an orange eaten the Chinese way
simply quartered or
sliced for a banquet
pieced together again

eating a Turkish orange
stripped of its rind
knifed into flat juicy rounds
sideways

Mexican orange inner skin
carved in ridges
on a rotating machine
devoured whole

an old man finds
a box of discarded orange halves
picks one up
sucks on it

in search of Chinese madness

red and green doors
opening to magic or sadness
let's go for a curry tart
shrimp dumplings
there's Chinese evergreen
blooming in the laundry window
rosewood cabinets sandalwood fans
salty balls sea horses
the ladies on the tea tins
carry baskets of snow pears
meet their lovers by the gate
hear the music of the abacus beads
the canary singing in the barbershop window
Chinatown is open tonight

the Mah-Jong players

under the halo
of a hanging lamp

yellow ivories
clacking in the night

tobacco fingers
build walls of China

circles birds flowers
swirling through the game

chopsticks

a memory of ivory chopsticks
first glimpse of China's landscape
waterfall and mountain
the three characters of our names
etched in red
the shame of chopsticks
brought by my mother
to the school lunchroom
a memory of being beaten
with chopsticks
the prophecy
a marriage far from home
because of fingers
held high on the chopsticks
lying in bed with a lover
like a pair of ivory chopsticks

Chinatown Sign

sweet olives
4 for 10¢

Cantonese Opera at Sun Sing Theater

diamonds glitter in black hair
the ass-length hair of the actresses
female and male impersonators
a red marriage bed behind curtains
straight beards to the waist
brocade and velvet
Cantonese puns
the visible curtain man
in white t-shirt and gray work pants
he is my favorite actor
offstage
a crazy shopping bag woman
smoking nervously
shaking her fat body
spraying fruit juice on the woman next to her
the man with a gun under his belt
a Hong Kong lady draped on the arm of her man
tape cassettes and medicine sold at intermission
the chilly white water fountains
the silver trunks of Lana Wong
Chinese jazz
I fall in love with the flute music
and of course
the rumble of the night train to Brooklyn

three peasant daughters

one wore glass bangles from Canton
nights she stepped out to dance

one fried almonds in salt
gave them away in glimmering jars

one looked out over blue water
dreaming of falling stars

Chinatown heartbreak

uncertain of the days to come
my heart gathers strength from
the echoes of your whistle like birdsong
nights when we shared one pillow
and you whispered ghost stories in my ear
nights when love lit up her lanterns

do you remember when it seemed
the whole world was closed
on shrimp gray days
the rain held us in
we saw Lincoln Center from a bus
elegance was a Greek restaurant
the New York Times was too big to fold
with too many dictionary words empty crosswords
they never reported the killing
down the street
the clothes they advertised were unreal too
who lounged who wore bathrobes
who had a dining room
everything in life being guesswork
cooking without teaspoons
eternal windowshoppers
we women were sometimes like children

wedding

wishes cover the red silk
Mai in a dress of brocade silk
glasses tinkle for a kiss of silk

bright as a hairpinned flower
the Chu women laugh and flower
to make of the feast one nightblooming flower

they want me to settle down
when I have not yet lived
mother talking to me in songs
of shopping bags and movie star calendars
given for free at the grocery store
(she wants a grandson)
with hopes of mooncakes dragon bracelets
and ginger soup
they want me to settle down
with the nice young man from Brooklyn
with the car and college degree
but every cockroach that runs across
my mind
whispers that I haven't seen Peking

Chinese New Year

Everytime I see something
Chinese, I think of you.
— ROBERT RIVERA, 13

see me on Sunday
ironing grandmother's dress
looking for chrysanthemums amid a profusion of oranges
wincing at the firecrackers on Chinatown's red streets

be me
playing pinball at Chinatown Fair
sampling sweets
happy with gifts the new year brings
not only red envelopes
but an open invitation for dinner on the Bowery
the presence of Chinese women talking about their lives
and more stories of the family

if you were here
I could toss three pennies to make you a hexagram
save you the last purple shrimp chip
make room for you at the table
as we feast for three nights

Chinese poem

since we last saw one another
the number of white strands in my hair has grown
one for each spring we've been apart
when will you again come to Chinatown
to feast on a bowl of noodles

lovers

once loved a man downtown
played the harmonica
sang Cantonese opera
dimples like pools of forgotten dreams

once loved a man uptown
had a black man's taste in music
steamed roast pork buns
loved me in an ancient way

Double Ten (10/10 day)

early morning
the Sunday sound of an accordion
a conversation with two Ukrainian women
about calling the plumber
taking baths in our kitchens
you like the green stone around my neck
later on the Bowery
black man strutting along
singing a Chinatown ballad
as I sing one of Billie's songs
in your kitchen warmer than mine
the strong smell of black mushrooms

For my grandfather's friend

they said you were a gambler
that you liked your drink too much
but it's the better moments that matter now
shining with your giving spirit
the times you called with Buddhist food
duck's feet a freshly killed chicken or
it might be for dinner at the association
to feast the advent of spring
the time we went shopping for simple things
warm underwear and a hat
the story in the hospital of
a boatride down the China coast to Hong Kong
when I caught a whiff of your seagoing spirit
it was Chinese New Year
the day you left the hospital
riding triumphant into Chinatown in a cab
"all roads lead to Chinatown"
the lion dancers and fireworks celebrated
your return to the coffee shop
where the workers spoke your name
I remember a back garden of my childhood
where small orange blossoms grew
I wonder are they flowering still

the middle daughter

how soft it felt
being cushioned in time between two sisters
one above and one below
following and being followed
a comfortable place to be

I am the second daughter
who should have been the first son
the one in the middle with many names
like Jong or Jongy
mixing Cantonese with English
now sometimes Paco or Panchita

I was that young child
with face shaped like a Chinese bun
the quietest baby with small feet
who became the most Chinese daughter
in gesture and style
who leaves home only to return again

winter festival

unearthing a new voice
shouting in Cantonese across the street
to my mother's Toishan friend
on her way home from the factory
a bit early
on this wintry feast night
speaking in teasing simple phrases
the only ones I know
your granddaughters so pretty
come eat rice with us
white balls of flour turning in its soup
our rice pot so full
its lid won't stay put

the magician growing bean sprouts
making baby soft breaking beancurd
listening to the tinkle of sugar
in the chrysanthemum tea
we tasted the roast pork buns
looking for the right one

For a lion dancer

beneath bright colors of a lion mask
a man in black silk
dances to a fierce beat of drums
a clash of cymbals
rhythm engraved on my heart's tissue
a dance that brings to me
my childhood in Chinatown
strike a strong lion's pose for me
dance into my life

cough remedy

a loving gesture
long forgotten
my mother rubbing
a piece of hot ginger
across my girlish chest
hard put to remember
the last time
I was so tickled

Chinese dentist

with your apartment
reeking of dirty diapers
acupuncture body
boxer shorts hung
in the shower
putting a red and white
striped screwdriver
into the mouth
of a terrified woman
hoping to save a few dollars

half a man

they got the best old food that
they ever had, in Chinatown . . .

—LEADBELLY

one cold Christmas night
two strangers trading sweet talk
at a bus stop
going to see my honey in Chinatown
hope she'll be there with something for me
won't you love me
I'll send you to driving school
we can drive to California
if you had a good man
you wouldn't be here
waiting for no damn bus

celebration

bravo for wondrous circumstance
born here yet breathing the air of another place
with the blood of independent silkwomen in my veins
different textures roll off my tongue
no telling what I might say

with the palm reader telling of
a past life in the Sudan
the coming of a favorite grandson
more worlds become possible

holding the power to dream in four languages
I enjoy being the exception to the rule
celebrate the one Asian American in the crowd

Pacific Avenue

Chinese voices fly up from the street
nudging me gently awake
like being home again dreaming poems

the old women in homespun tam o'shanters
move through Tai Chi Chuan
elegant and timeless

sun and bay window draw out the poem
in silk threads of
white sails and crescent moon

young girls on the corner
selling bags of garlic
even the vegetables take on new forms

Chinatown, San Francisco

oldtimers play pinball to quicken the heart
bachelors in the doughnut shop sip dreams
seek solace in homecooked platters
found only in restaurants
old men talk of Tai Chi in the park
chess games in Portsmouth Square
you are a sight for sore eyes
I am in a state of reverie

donde se venden pavos

old woman from El Salvador
in search of turkey on
the streets of Chinatown
someone to speak Spanish with
we meet at a bus stop
talk about the weather family
the killings in your country
sobrina nieta hermano matanzas
I tell you in so many words
you are on a wild goose chase
the Chinese do not eat much turkey
warm smiles and always the parting
que le vaya bien

Mount Tamalpais

a picnic for all soothing times
a Chinese American picnic
sesame cakes pickled mustard greens
turnip cakes bean sprout rolls
quickly vanish
to the dismay of a bee
with a craving for Chinese food
a bed of clouds
Mount Diablo Angel Island
white pinpoints sailing on a bay
that could be sky
lovers rub suntan oil on one another
lovers in the shade of a tree
discuss the meaning of passion
dancers silhouetted on the hillside
I read a book of poems in a wheatlike meadow

the great American yellow poem

she heard tales about saving grapefruit skins for cooking
she grew bright under the neon dragon of Chinatown
she made saffron curry rice for friends
she attended a barbecue in Amarillo, Texas
she stepped around yellow piss in snow
she cut herself on a Hawaiian pineapple
she learned to name forsythia where it grew
visions of ochre and citronella eluded her

fruit mutations

grape approaching lichee
peach approaching mango

México

the smell of tortillas and cilantro
the largest mango
small crabs digging holes in the sand
white shells in the form of breasts with brown nipples
yellow and lavender houses
a favorite word "golondrina" painted on a boat
Tai Chi on the beach
breakfast in a place swarming with flies
country love songs on the jukebox
papaya and almond trees
the Mexican night
fresh smell of el campo
luciérnagas

recuerdos de la
chinita en Guatemala

the call of chinita
the sound of Cantonese
fish tank
the comfort of jasmine tea
sound of a cleaver chopping
I dream of rice and beans
give away my Chinese fan

Guatemala

two babies sitting in the doorway of the hotel
chewing on pieces of bread
Evelyn's father
gray haired with twinkling eyes plays
let me call you sweetheart
on the guitar
he talks of New York San Francisco
Boston and the Charles
we dance the foxtrot
se prohibe dormir en estas ruinas
birds singing their hearts away
bundles of Indian children sleeping in the plaza
folded into blankets by 7:30
in the cobblestone streets
a freckled girl asks me to open a jar for her
on the road to Chimaltenango
a man sitting behind me slurping a mango
carrying a large bunch of white flowers
woman washing her clothes on the beach
the water is green and gray
the young waiter in the empty hotel
sells me two comic books
el valiente
they are old and smell of rain
in the market
I have my fortune told by a bird
picking out a piece of colored tissue paper
an Indian woman teases me about finding a husband
discs of homemade chocolate

babies wearing red hats tied at the top
hung with trinkets and coins
chunks of white cheese placed on banana leaves
young girls with brown cracked hands
clear stone earrings
people ask for the time
so they can hear my voice
the sign on one doorway
se venden tortillas

adios, vaya con dios

For my students

(scene:
  at the Midnight Candy store
  a favorite song
  always and forever by Heat Wave
  playing on a sound box
  raising love to a new high)

if I could leave you without tears
I would leave you with
a chill pill for tomorrow's worries
a kiss on each cheek to soften the blows

cradle song for Mieko

dark-eyed baby
coral hatted Mieko
slurping at your mama's breast
before your evening sleep
mama's in the kitchen folding dumplings
papa's making you a loft bed
so pillow your sweet baby head
dreaming of golden bracelets
green tea
a home in the country

tulips

in crayon gardens
children plant tulips
magenta and violet

in Amsterdam along the canals
of the red light district
tulips in bloom

in a New Yorker cartoon
an artist sketches tulips
for a brownstone window

tulip cup tulip
lamp tulip tree
tulips in bloom

we are sailing off
the coast of Portugal

your love, sail white,
a virgin line of verse

and a lovely drunkenness
washes over me

ode to a patchwork quilt

hanging delicately on the wall
neglected in the rush of days
for now you've become
subject of my poetic concern

wondering of the patient hands
that pieced you together
the forgotten grandmothers and rockers
how squarely you've framed nature

>   a fisherboy with straw hat
>   a spider web
>   the crescent moon
>   maple leaves
>   ladies' fans and hand mirrors
>   the monogram H for
>   Harriet heaven home

hanging in a small room in the city
the cat reaches for your velvet
your stitches tell
the romance of autumn upcountry
the aura of times no longer

night light

on the coral night lamp
a pattern of stars
small beauty floods the room

purple poem

shades of lilac and lavender
think of all the purple times in your life
unusual moments like the
black purple of grapeskins and eggplants
the purple gray of summer plums
the unexpected purple of bruises
the dark purple of a trailing ivy
turn back to a purple childhood
filled with violet delicacy
taste Welch's jelly jawbreakers
the fear of purple people eaters
purple words crazy purple sneakers
best of all in springtime
the making of purple
rubbing the bodies of
two mollusks together
by the light of the full moon

love's canopy
turned into a
can of peas

found Chinese poem, 1944

mango bird
pendants, tinkling jingles
3-cornered dumplings
hole in door for cat
sweet spirit of rice

love song

a young Chinese scholar writes
was it by the goldfish pond
I first noticed
the dark beauty of your braids
the gentle song of your voice
the garden of peonies in your dress
was it by the Pearl River

Sa Gow

in my father's village in China
a country woman washed vegetables
by a stream and stone bridge
peanuts lay drying in the sun

a country woman washed vegetables
as we walked in umbrella shade
peanuts lay drying in the sun
on the dirt road to my father's house

as we walked in umbrella shade
cousins and aunts turned and smiled
on the dirt road to my father's house
our relatives in a procession

cousins and aunts turned and smiled
a shy girl asked for a pretty skirt
our relatives in a procession
I found a circle of kin

a shy girl asked for a pretty skirt
a young woman wanted an American husband
I found a circle of kin
posing for a proud portrait

a young woman wanted an American husband
by a stream and stone bridge
posing for a proud portrait
in my father's village in China

China

on West Lake
the languid willows
hang their silk sleeves
along the poet's path
wisteria blossoms lotus leaves
watermelon eaters on the street
crouching in the dark

scenes gathered from a
Chinese-English dictionary

clouds clearing away
simple clothing
rose-flower cake
coral chopsticks
night shining pearl
to gaze at the ocean and sigh
third day after a child's birth
moon clouded over
to give rice to the poor
husband of a wife's younger sister
to lie down undressed and sigh constantly
lunar mansion
to hold the knees and sing away
throw an embroidered ball in choosing a husband
to drown infants
first woman who taught Chinese people how to make silk
    from silkworm
unknown hero born in the country
to enjoy chrysanthemums
fireflies at the window and snow on the table
with as many children as grasshoppers
anti-mosquito incense
incense sticks indicating time
double pillow used by newly married people
silence of three minutes
embroidered robes with axes drawn on them in black and
    white
beautiful girl from a lower family

bamboo chair for mountain traveler
small open basket for holding rice
the yellow carp
white jasmine
kneel while incense burns
fried dough strips
a Buddhist word
bound feet of woman
to play at Chinese chess
a Taoist priest's robe
worms in books, clothes, or wood
carry dish with hands
songs of stilt walkers
overfed baby vomits
coconut shell as ladle
to rub Chinese ink
whitish jade ear-plugs
a stroke to the right in writing
take off slipper
my dull mind is suddenly opened

one Chinese apple
my love with as many seeds
take small crimson bites

OTHER POEMS

Although not part of either "Crazy Melon" or "Chinese Apple," there is a small number of poems that Frances Chung sometimes included in manuscripts she submitted to fellowship competitions or anthologies and periodicals. Six such poems appear in the present section, only one of which, "Chinese Women," has been published before. The poem that begins with the one-word line "chaúl" was part of Chung's application, dated June 10, 1977, for a Creative Artists Program Service fellowship administered by the New York State Council on the Arts (NYSCA). "poem for an Indian scholar" was part of an eight-poem manuscript that Chung sent in August 1978 to Quincey Troupe to be considered for publication in his journal, American Rag; *the other seven poems are all included in either "Crazy Melon" or "Chinese Apple." "kaleidoscope" and "Chinese Women" were submitted along with several other poems to the special "Without Ceremony" issue of the journal* Ikon *(2nd series 9 [1988]), organized by the Asian Women United Journal Collective. Guest poetry editor Kimiko Hahn chose "Chinese Women" and the untitled poem that begins "since we last saw one another . . ." for publication; the latter appears in "Crazy Melon" under the title "Chinese poem." "marriage signs" and "American actress (1907–1961)" were part of another grant application made to NYSCA by Chung, ca. 1987–88.*

chaúl
blue
Chinese
silk

poem for an Indian scholar

a friend sent me a book of Asian love poems
'coloured stars'
with the poem
'black hair'
I like to think it is a rare copy
found in a secondhand bookshop

we are the only Asian teachers in school
perhaps the only poets in the building
so that during a free moment
we can take private journeys
away from our lessons and children

the sight of me combing my long hair
brings you back to your country
where you tell me
girls sit in the open air
combing each other's hair

I too wish for India
riding on a swing
like the girl in the postcard
it is from you that I learn a new sound
'Gitanjali'

you urge me to sit by a window
on a rainy day
and write poems
I wonder is it that easy

kaleidoscope

Chinatown
my Chinese kaleidoscope
tube of ten thousand flowers
hibiscus orchids orange blossoms
father and son delight
in a pair of goldfish
women gathering gingko nuts in Central Park
tiny yellow flowers tucked in the marketplace
good enough to eat
my first taste of dried persimmons
the very fruit grandmother gave mother
for her sea voyage to America
when the Chinese evergreen flowers
tie a red bow around it

Chinese Women

old woman at a window
sitting to the side like a cat sunning herself
seeing life in all its tawdriness and splendor on 14 street
the lights shine on you
an icon
jade and yellow gold on your fingers and ears
while behind you there is only dark space

today it has been raining cats dogs pitchforks
your place by the window is empty
I am missing you
a stranger

I sing to myself a child's song
we used to chant on days like this about
big rains flooding the streets and younger sister
hiding under the bed in her flowered slippers

> lok dai yu
> ser jum gai
> mui mui nay mui
> chong ha di
> jerk fa hai

one out of every four persons on this earth is chinese
still there are times when you feel alone
I hope your reverie and view
do not leave you unhappy

marriage signs

two incense sticks burn as one
you drink the tea I pour for you

American actress (1907–1961)

Anna May Wong
L. A. laundry child
phoenix woman
sea green silk gown
ivory cigarette holder
solitary player
on a fast train
through China
speaking Chinese
with American accent

COMMENTARY

By *Walter K. Lew*

4

in the museum of the ancient book
pi sheng made prints in clay from 1041 to 1049
dinging in la gran muralla china
fish tank
one girl looks chinese
chinese paintings on the walls
the waitress asks me if i want 'palitos'
áññll antigua veiled in a mist
still streets
a chinese baby
jasmine tea to comfort me
its familiar clear taste
chinese là calendar
jukebox music
a chinese melon
the sound of the cleaver chopping
woman wishes me que le vaya bien
in dark streets
the men still call me ' chinita bonita'
crickets chirping
bundles of indian children sleeping in the ▮▮▮▮ plaza
enfolded completely in blankets at 7?30
i dream of rice and beans

Page from the rough draft of an unfinished poem by Frances Chung.

ABOUT THE TEXT

Frances Chung conceived of most of her poems as being precisely arranged into book-length manuscripts. To be sure, the echoing and development of themes, diction, and imagery must have attracted her—the effect of both a larger framework (always shifting, of course, its crazy melodic) and the unpredictability of individual poems within it. But she also enjoyed the manual process of bookmaking. In an interview with the artist Tomie Arai, Chung related that she took pleasure in typing fresh copies of her poems and that she had made her own "paperback book" out of folded sheets of paper.[1] One collation, or part of one, survives among Chung's papers, and one version of the "Crazy Melon" manuscript was neatly preserved on six-by-eight-inch loose-leaf sheets in a transparent plastic box, her Chinese seal impressed in red on the title page and a colorful plum candy wrapper taped onto the box's lid. It would appear that Chung deliberately mimicked a standard set of book dimensions and that it was a way of partially materializing her oft-mentioned hope of bringing her own book into the world.

Given Chung's care for authenticating her own texts, it is all the more important to confirm that the pieces brought together in the present volume are those that, at certain points in her life, she indeed wished to publish. This is the main purpose of the following notes.

The Selection of Manuscripts and Their Chronology

The present volume comprises two previously unpublished book manuscripts, titled "Crazy Melon" and "Chinese

Apple," and a brief third section of six other poems selected from manuscripts that Chung herself submitted to journals, anthologies, or fellowship competitions. Whereas preliminary plans for the book at another publisher were solely based on versions of "Crazy Melon," the present volume's inclusion of the more recently discovered "Chinese Apple" manuscript yields a richer conception of the scope and achievement of Chung's writing. Much gratitude, indeed, is owed the Chung family, especially Frances Chung's older sister Edna, for giving generous access to the poet's papers and for its support of the project's development into a more comprehensive form.

"Crazy Melon"

In an autobiographical note found among her papers, Chung revealed that she had "written a secret book entitled Crazy Melon." Stating on its dedication page that the book is "For the Chinatown people," and imprinted with Chung's own ink seal, "Crazy Melon" is a collection of poetry, prose poems, and prose vignettes largely set in New York Chinatown and other parts of the Lower East Side. The book is not explicitly divided into sections, but much of it is organized according to brief, unstated series of themes and images, such as recounted dreams, broken love affairs, tedium at the workplace, wandering through various neighborhoods, and fantasies of Chinese American warriorship. It includes some of Chung's earliest work, such as "bread," of which there is a December 1968 draft, and the poem beginning "he was growing old," one version of which is dated December 1970. Some of these poems, then, were written while Chung was still in her late teens or early twenties.[2]

Chung's autobiographical note does not reflect the inclusion of her poems in the anthologies *Ordinary Women* and *American Born and Foreign*, published in 1978 and 1979, respectively, despite mentioning earlier, less widely distributed publications, such as *Yellow Pearl* and the journal *Bridge*.[3] From this omission we can conclude that at least a preliminary version of "Crazy Melon" existed by 1978. In fact, the compilation of *Ordinary Women* must already have been completed by the summer of 1977, when Adrienne Rich wrote an introduction for the book that quotes from Chung's poetry.[4] It is safe, therefore, to push the date of "Crazy Melon" back to mid-1977, at the latest.

To judge from the handwritten numbering at the bottom of each page, what I take to be the latest "Crazy Melon" manuscript, which I arbitrarily call ms. C, originally consisted of eighty-two pages, but is presently missing seven folios: pages 8 [10], 31–32 [33], 55 [57], and 78–80 [79–81].[5] It also contains sixteen poems that are *not* included in the other two versions of "Crazy Melon" extant in Chung's papers (mss. A and B). For a detailed listing of the poems included in mss. A–C, see the appendix to this section.

A strong argument for the C ms., included in the present book as the version that Chung most likely intended to publish, is the almost completely consistent typing and formatting of its text, indicating that it was meant to be read by a relatively "professional" editor or critic. The highly inconsistent formatting of mss. A and B, on the other hand, give the impression that they were assembled from pieces typed at widely different times for various purposes.

As for the poems I have interposed for the missing pages, I am confident that pages 8 [10], 31–32 [33], 55 [57], and one page (the poem titled "three minds") of pages 78–80 [79–81] are correctly restored since there is almost no variation in sequence between the three versions, even before and after the points at which the sixteen additional poems of ms. C are inserted. Except for pages 78–80 [79–81] the order of pieces both preceding and following the lacunae is identical in all three manuscripts, suggesting that the C ms.'s missing pieces are the same as the ones that occur in the corresponding positions in mss. A and B, except, of course, for textual revisions Chung may have made (see appendix).

As for pages 78–80 [79–81], I have: (i) inserted the poem that begins "And if I said 'ming' to you" because it is unexpectedly absent from the spot corresponding to its location in mss. A and B (after the poem that begins "that stiff figure there") and I see no grounds for arguing that, aside from the A ms. poem that begins "And when I want to make," it was the only poem dropped in the transition to ms. C; (ii) inserted a page indicating a "Missing Poem"; (iii) inserted the poem "of three minds" on the basis of analogy with mss. A and B, in which it served as the final and penultimate piece respectively. For this group of three pages alone, the sequence of interposed pieces is admittedly speculative.

It is also unknown whether or not ms. C concluded with a glossary, as do the A and B mss. I have just the same included it as "Crazy Melon"'s closing page—thus suggesting that the C ms. is also lacking its page 83.

Another challenge that the "Crazy Melon" mss. presented was devising a uniform way of deciding, for purposes of typesetting style, whether certain pieces are poetry or prose. In the absence of right-margin justification, indentation to begin new paragraphs is perhaps the most unambiguous sign that a piece should be set as prose. In ms. C only four pieces meet this strict criterion. If, however, one returns to the earlier A ms., there are twelve with paragraph indentation, confirming the sense that certain pieces, such as the reminiscence that begins "We spent summer afternoons catching . . . ," are prose poems or vignettes.[6] All of these have been set in the present book as prose, though without restoring indentation from the A ms.

This nonetheless leaves certain pieces treated as poetry even though they read like prose, such as the one that begins "Chinese New Year. Yellow chrysanthemums . . ." Indeed, comparisons between the A and C manuscripts' versions of such pieces reveal numerous differences in line breaks, implying, at first glance, that they are arbitrary. To my eye, however, Chung, especially near the conclusions of some of her prose poems, was often writing in a form that dissolved the difference between the two genres: they were prose in which the grouping of particular words together within one line, often the final one, was meaningful and deliberate, whether in terms of imagery, semantics, prosody, or phonetics, as is the case in poetry. Thus, rather than rely on my own erratic sense of the presence or absence of enjambment, I have decided to err on the side of replicating Chung's own typing: each line break in ms. C is accurately reproduced—except in the case of the aforementioned twelve pieces that, in at least one of the three versions of "Crazy Melon," use paragraph indentation.

"Chinese Apple"

"Chinese Apple" is the title of the typewritten forty-eight-poem manuscript that Chung submitted to the Walt Whitman Award competition sponsored by the Academy of American Poets in New York City. Including the cover and title pages, it comprised a total of fifty-two pages. Since part of the Walt Whitman Award is book publication of the manuscript, there is ample reason for presenting "Chinese Apple" as a separate collection, not just an ad hoc assemblage or sample. The orderly sequence of themes and reservation of the title poem for its final page reinforce the sense of a coherently arranged manuscript.

"Chinese Apple," unlike "Crazy Melon," contains no prose poems or vignettes, and it could be suggested that this is one perhaps negative consequence of the manuscript being prepared for a conventional poetry competition. However, I want to emphasize that "Chinese Apple" is by no means a mere excerpt from or reduction of "Crazy Melon." Only five of "Chinese Apple"'s forty-eight poems appear in "Crazy Melon," and much of "Chinese Apple" either cultivates new themes, such as tributes to classical Chinese literature (given all the more significance by the choice of "For Li Po" as the opening poem), or attempts new formal experiments, as in the pantoum "Sa Gow."[7]

Neither the manuscript nor the card from the Academy informing Chung that she had not been given the award is dated, and the Academy does not keep records of submissions for more than two years. However, "For Li Po" refers to students reading "Pound's translation" at the New School for Social Science Research, where Chung attended writing classes in 1979 and 1980, perhaps allowing us to infer that the collection is more recent than at least the earliest "Crazy Melon" manuscript, which, as argued above, was compiled no later than mid-1977.[8]

More extensive evidence that "Chinese Apple" was compiled after "Crazy Melon" can be adduced from significant shifts in the composition of the poetry samples that Chung submitted in 1977, 1980, and 1987 as part of applications for Creative Artists Program Service (CAPS) and Writer-in-Residence fellowships administered by the New York State Council on the Arts (NYSCA).[9] In the earliest application, dated June 10, 1977, nine out of the total of twenty-four poems appear only in "Crazy Melon," nine are from "Chinese Apple," and five do not appear in either manuscript.[10] The nine selections from "Crazy Melon" tend to preserve the order of their appearance in the "secret book"; for instance, the first six poems of the application sample are the thirty-ninth, fortieth, fifty-fifth to fifty-seventh, and sixty-second poems of ms. C, respectively. This is not the case with the poems that eventually appeared in the "Chinese Apple" manuscript, suggesting that in 1977 "Crazy Melon" was much closer to its final organization than "Chinese Apple" was—if, in fact, the latter existed yet in even a rudimentary form.

Three years later in 1980, however, the twenty-two-poem sample Chung submitted with another CAPS fellowship application includes just two poems from "Crazy Melon" and nineteen from "Chinese Apple."[11] Finally, in Chung's successful 1987 application to NYSCA to be writer-in-residence at the Henry St. Settlement, only one of the twenty poems is from "Crazy Melon" (but it is one that also appears in "Chinese Apple"), seventeen are included only in "Chinese Apple," and the two remaining selections are part of neither manuscript.[12] Of course, these drastic shifts do not prove that all or even most of the poems in "Chinese Apple" were *written* after those included in "Crazy Melon," but they do demonstrate that sometime after mid-1977 and no later than 1980 Chung came to prefer them as representations of her work, although they were probably not yet arranged in a sequence like the one submitted to the Walt Whitman Award competition.

Other Poems

Information on the six poems in this section has already been given (p. 138). Chung left behind other accomplished or intriguing pieces, and some of these may eventually be published once the present book has had time to find an audience and spread knowledge of Chung's better writing.

Notes

1. Tape-recorded interview, 1989.

2. The earliest dated pieces I have found among Chung's papers were written in 1967. Chung was born in New York City on September 5, 1950, and passed away from rare complications after surgery on December 8, 1990.

3. In chronological order: *Yellow Pearl* (New York: Basement Workshop, 1972), p. 19; *Bridge: An Asian American Perspective* 3.4 (February 1975): 9, and 3.6 (August 1975): 28; Sara Miles, Patricia Jones, Sandra Maria Esteves, and Fay Chiang, eds., *Ordinary Women, An Anthology of Poetry by New York City Women*, introduction by Adrienne Rich (New York: Ordinary Women, 1978), pp. 31–36; Fay Chiang, Helen Wong Huie, Jason Hwang, Richard Oyama, and Susan L. Yung, eds., *American Born and Foreign, An Anthology of Asian American Poetry*, special double issue of *Sunbury, A Poetry Magazine* 7–8 (Bronx, N.Y.: 1979), pp. 15, 47–48, 103–4, 121–22, 140. Both *Ordinary Women* and *American Born and Foreign* are mentioned by Chung in a subsequent fellowship application dated May 30, 1980.

4. "There are many different voices here; there is also one voice. 'Ordinary women' finding their connections with other women, with the blind prostitutes in Hong Kong, the shopping-bag woman in Union Square, the sisters in prison (who are also writing poems); making through poetry the connections with self which mean survival. As more and more women of every tongue and color affirm these connections, hope also grows for the strength and wisdom to move, *embrace difference as identity as key*, break loose and transform the cities." (Adrienne Rich, introduction to Sara Miles et al, eds., *Ordinary Women*, pp. 9–10; emphasis in the original.) The phrase "the blind prostitutes in Hong Kong" is a reference to an untitled poem by Chung that was included in *Ordinary Women* (p. 35) and appears here as part of "Crazy Melon"; its first line is "Walking along the Bowery, can't."

5. Page numbers refer to numbers written at the bottom of each page of the original C ms. while numbers enclosed in brackets refer to the present book.

6. Most of the difference between the A and C mss. in regard to indentation is due to the fact that in the latter ms. the opening lines of single-paragraph pieces, such as the one that begins "Goofy Lala was the wicked woman who . . . ," are not indented.

7. The five poems that appear in both "Crazy Melon" and "Chinese Apple" are the ones that begin "do you remember when it seemed . . . ," "they want me to settle down . . . ," and "the magician growing bean sprouts . . . ," and the two entitled "fruit mutations" and "scenes gathered from a Chinese-English dictionary." These poems are presented in both sections of the present book in order to keep Chung's intended sequences intact.

8. Among the literature courses and workshops that Chung took upon

returning to New York after earning a B.A. in Mathematics from Smith College (1971) were two at the New School: Colette Inez's "The Craft of Poetry" (1979) and Gilbert Sorrentino's "Writing Poetry" (1980). She also took poetry workshops led by Lawson Fusao Inada and Mei-mei Berssenbrugge at the Basement Workshop in Chinatown. Later, she herself taught poetry workshops at the Poetry Project at St. Mark's Church in-the-Bowery and at the Chatham Square and Seward Park branches of the New York City Public Library.

9. Chung was awarded a CAPS poetry fellowship for 1980–81 and a 1987–88 Writer-in-Residence grant.

10. In addition, the poem that begins "scenes gathered from a Chinese-English dictionary" is the final poem of the sample and appears in both "Crazy Melon" and "Chinese Apple."

11. Again, "scenes gathered from a Chinese-English dictionary" appears in both "Crazy Melon" and "Chinese Apple," but what had been the first line in the 1977 application's version of the poem is its title in the 1980 application, as in the "Chinese Apple" version.

12. These two poems, "marriage signs" and "American actress (1907–1961)," are published for the first time in the "Other Poems" section of the present book.

Appendix

Composition of the Main "Crazy Melon" Manuscripts

The following table lists each piece that appears in the A, B, and C ms. versions of "Crazy Melon" found among Frances Chung's papers. As I have explained in the "About the Text" essay, the significantly longer C ms. is probably the latest version and the one that Chung most intended to publish. In the table's B and C ms. columns, "Y" indicates that the piece appears in the exact same form, wording, and sequential location as it does in the A ms., "y" that it appears with some textual alteration, and "N" that the piece in the A ms. does not appear at all. The opening lines of untitled pieces are enclosed in square brackets. Page numbers given in the C ms. column reflect those handwritten at the bottom of each ms. page. Not counting the title and dedication pages and glossary, the A ms. consists of sixty pieces typed on sixty-nine pages and the B ms. sixty pieces on sixty-seven pages, while the extant parts of ms. C comprise seventy pieces, numbered out to page 82, but with pages 8 [10], 31–32 [33], 55 [57], and 78–80 [79–81] missing.

A ms.	B ms.	C ms.
(Title page)	Y	y
(Dedication page)	Y	y
[Yo vivo en el barrio chino]	Y	Y
[The echoes of the night trucks]	Y	Y
	—	[References to your home as a ghetto. Ancient]
[No one uses words such as]	Y	Y
[welcome to Chinatown ladies and gentlemen]	Y	Y

[One black boy on a class trip]	Y	Y
[Neon lights that warm no one. How]	Y	y
[The movie theater filled with sticky]	Y	N (p. 8 [10])
—	—	[Philodendron plants. Monk's food and]
—	—	[They dress alike and cut their black hair into]
[They are seen in different]	y	Y
[The hare krishna people come]	Y	Y
[Walking along the Bowery, can't]	y	Y
bread	Y	Y
—	—	bread #2
—	—	surrealists on east houston
[There are more Chinese bums]	Y	Y
[Aside from the trees in Columbus Park]	Y	Y
[it is the same walk]	Y	Y
[oh lucky me]	y	Y
—	—	[On New Year's Eve we throw the]
[Chinese New Year. Yellow]	y	y
[the winter wind sits in the living room]	Y	Y
[a flower lifts on Mott Street]	Y	Y
[The summer nights we spent on the cool]	y	y
[We stole a snail from the]	y	y

157

A ms.	B ms.	C ms. (*Continued*)
[Goofy Lala was the wicked]		y
[We spent summer afternoons catching]		y
[My Italian girlfriends dressed]		y
[On Saturday, it is 14 Street for]		y
[Every Sunday, we go to 'Jew Street',]		N (pp. 31–32 [33])
[Mango did not know what she wanted.]	Y	y
[Please don't tell me you're sorry.]	Y	y
——	——	[in a corner of the subway door discovered]
——	——	[mosquito]
Lessons of Violence	Y	y
[It would have been nice if people saw]	Y	y
Piropos de la chinita	Y	Y
[the magician growing bean sprouts]	Y	Y
[they want me to settle down]	Y	Y
[There is a group of]	y	y
[this Chinese warrior]	Y	Y
[that Zen time in the snow]	Y	Y
——	——	dream collection
[Discovery of the secret power to]	y[1]	Y

[The cockroach dream nightmare. Banging]	Y	Y
—	—	[behind the chatter]
—	—	[We use newspaper for a]
[And when I want to make]	y	N
[Where is the cockroach who left]	Y	Y
[Don't leave any rice in your]	Y	Y
[When the water in the pot is]	Y	Y
[If it is true that you are what you]	Y	Y
[I am fruit crazy. I love six]	y	N (p. 55 [57])
Fruit Mutations	Y	Y
[I have very little]	Y	Y
[do you remember when it seemed the whole world]	Y	Y
[Lunchtime at the factory is a family]	y	y
—	—	[I discover the other women in my family. My]
[Sitting across from me on the bus a]	Y	y
[Riding the subway is an adventure]	Y	Y
[he was growing old]	Y	Y
—	—	[I call her the tea lady (to myself) because I]
[He wears a uniform of red and black]	y	Y
Beekman Hospital	Y	y
[He came down the hall with blackness in his]	y	y

A ms.	B ms.	C ms. (*Continued*)
[that stiff figure there]	Y	Y
[And if I said "ming" to you]	Y[2]	N[3]
	—	[viet nam]
Taiwan	Y	Y
Hong Kong	Y	Y
[I went to sleep last]	Y	y
	—	[The young man dressed in white is a barber at]
[En busca del barrio chino en Lima . . .]	Y[4]	Y (p. 77 [78])
of three minds	y[5]	N[6]
	—	[scenes gathered from a Chinese–English dictionary:] (pp. 81–82 [82–83])
Glossary	Y	N[7]

1. In the B ms. this piece and the immediately following "[The cockroach dream nightmare. Banging]" are transposed.
2. In the B ms. this poem appears between "[I went to sleep last]" and "[En busca del barrio chino en Lima . . .]."
3. No pagination gap. I have interposed this poem as p. 78 [79] of ms. C.
4. In the B ms., "[En busca del barrio chino en Lima . . .]" and the immediately following "of three minds" are transposed.
5. See preceding note.
6. I have interposed this poem as p. 80 [81] of ms. C.
7. I have added the glossary as a concluding p. 83 [84] of ms. C.

AFTERWORD
A. Paper Clips

The discourse of the city is a syncretic discourse, political in its untranslatability. Hence the language of the state elides it. Unable to speak all the city's languages, unable to speak all at once, the state's language becomes monumental, the silence of headquarters, the silence of the bank. . . . Between the night workers and the day workers lies the interface of light; in the rotating shift, the disembodiment of lived time. The walkers of the city travel at different speeds, their steps the handwriting of a personal mobility.

—SUSAN STEWART, *On Longing*

> The echoes of the night trucks
> bouncing off the cobblestones
> on Canal Street play on the
> silences in my bones. Playing
> games with the red and green
> light on the corner of Mott and
> Canal, we find an excuse to run—
> we who know that those who are
> brave cross Mott Street on a
> diagonal.
>
> —"CRAZY MELON"

> Yo vivo en el barrio chino
> de Nueva York.
>
> —"CRAZY MELON"

Frances Chung's poetry crossed New York Chinatown on many diagonals, each one summoning a different kind of courage.

What she returned to after her college years in New England was already the "new," "reconstructed" Chinatown: a situation that made her writing about childhood both invaluable and always more belated.

The courage to begin a book "for the Chinatown people" in Spanish, opening her claim to turf with the statement "Yo vivo en el barrio chino / de Nuevo York . . ." A *barrio*: exactly the profile (ghetto, slum, *kampong*, "capital-scarce, deteriorated urban terrain"[1]) that tens of millions were spent to eradicate.

The courage to dedicate "Crazy Melon" to a community largely unable to read it.

"An interlingual poetics would change the shapes and sounds of dominant languages like English by pushing the language to its limit and breaking it open or apart. The interpenetration of languages . . . allows us to re-imagine these languages and cultures not as discrete entities, but as radically relational."[2] In light of Chung's deft zigzag through linguistic zones, she should be seen as an early master of "interlingual" Asian American poetics, a distinction that has been largely accorded to Theresa Hak Kyung Cha, whose time in New York temporarily coincided with hers.[3] As Chung herself stated, "In my poetry, I play with images from the Chinese and Spanish languages," and one of the workshops she taught was on "trilingual poetry."[4] Her writing juxtaposes the languages of the Lower East Side, perhaps for future readers like the many bilingual students she taught yet another language to—mathematics—in J.H.S. 22 on Columbia Street, Murray Bergtraum High School on Pearl, and Dr. Sun Yat Sen Intermediate on Hester Street, from 1973 onward.

Our late knowledge of Chung's work was due to more than her early death, the years it took to find an appropriate publisher, or the absence of her work from any trade-marketed multicultural, Asian American, or feminist anthology.[5] Though hidden by the apparent immediacy of her poems—their confiding voice, whimsical parallels and compact narratives and tableaux—belatedness lies at the heart of Chung's poetics. It anticipates (learns intensely from early disappointment) missed communication despite every effort to be clear and sympathetic, to cultivate a listening voice.[6]

Unlike the work of two other remarkable poets of New York Chinatown during the nascence of the Asian American cultural and political movement of the late 1960s and early '70s—Fay Chiang and Wing Tek Lum—Chung's poetics, by maintaining planes of a paradoxically *untranslatable equivalence* between languages ("of three minds," "And if I said 'ming' to you," "scenes from a Chinese-English dictionary"), perpetuates doubt as to whether the volatile meanings swirling about her particular position among languages, communities, and formidable social and political forces can ever be brought to unity, to historical harmony. The exception to this, though Chung acknowledges its limits, is her erotic poetry, which sexualizes cross-cultural exchanges (of politics, food, music, and fashion across ethnic lines), adapts High Modernist Orientalism to her own local purposes (Pound's and Kenneth Rexroth's translations seem especially influential), and sensuously displaces images of interracial sexuality ("dream collection," "Double Ten (10/10 day)").

Chung's poetry is filled with questions, but not question marks:

> I remember a back garden of my childhood
> where small orange blossoms grew
> I wonder are they flowering still
>
> would you answer
> would you hear me
>
> was it by the Pearl River

For in her work every phrase inquires, is a reaching (for remembrance, distant history, or the meanings of words from languages never completely acquired): not to be answered so much as followed into new views and derivations.

•

it took me a lifetime to learn the Chinese for paper clip now
the image is mine forever holder of ten thousand words let
us paper clip together

     —Frances Chung, for her trilingual poetry workshop

B. *Vis à vis the* Surrealist Poetics *of Nishiwaki Junzaburō* *(1929)*

Poetry is a method of calling one's attention to . . . banal re-
ality by means of a certain unique interest (a mysterious
sense of exaltation). (NJ 5[7])

> Where is the cockroach who left
> its footprint on my bowl?

A hypothesis: The realm of poetry expands infinitely and fi-
nally disappears. As a corollary (*ipso facto*) of this hypothesis
the following rule is set forth: The most expanded, the most
advanced mode of poetry is that which is closest to its own
extinction. (NJ 20)

> chaúl
> blue
> Chinese
> silk

Things that do not symbolize attract us more. (NJ 153)

> Chinatown Sign
>
> sweet olives
> 4 for 10¢

It is dangerous to discuss poetry. I have already fallen off
the cliff. (NJ 19)

C. From Frances Chung's Library

The Selected Poems of Federico Garcia Lorca. Ed. Francisco Garcia Lorca and Donald M. Allen; various translators.
Picture Bride, Cathy Song.
No More Masks! An Anthology of Poems by Women. Ed. Florence Howe and Ellen Bass.
The New American Poetry, 1945–1960. Ed. Donald M. Allen.
Five Decades, A Selection (Poems 1925–1970), Pablo Neruda. Ed., trans., Ben Belitt.
Sunflower Splendor. Ed. Wu-chi Liu and Irving Yucheng Lo.
Cold Mountain, 100 Poems by the T'ang Poet Han-shan. Trans. Burton Watson.
Translations from the Chinese. Trans. Arthur Waley.
Li Ch'ing-chao. Complete Poems. Trans. Kenneth Rexroth and Ling Chung.
One Robe, One Bowl. Trans. John Stevens.
ABC of Reading and *Selected Poems*, Ezra Pound.
The Complete Poems of Charles Reznikoff, Vol. 1 and 2.
Selected Poems, Kenneth Patchen.
Emergency Poems, Nicanor Parra. Trans. Miller Williams.
Sun 4.2 (Spring 1975).
New Poetry of Mexico. Selected with notes by Octavio Paz and others, ed. Mark Strand.
Quite Early One Morning, Dylan Thomas.
One Hundred More Poems from the Japanese. Trans. Kenneth Rexroth.
If You Want to Know What We Are: A Carlos Bulosan Reader. Ed. E. San Juan, Jr.
Home to Stay, Asian American Women's Fiction. Ed. Sylvia Watanabe and Carol Bruchac.
Taking to Water: Poems, Roberta Spear.
Amplitude, Tess Gallagher.
Where Water Comes Together with Other Water, Raymond Carver.
Mystery and detective novels by Sue Grafton, Elmore Leonard, Marcia Muller, and Robert Van Gulik (The "Judge Dee" series). Short stories by Anne Beattie and Ethan Canin. William Carlos Williams.[8]

In an unpublished piece, Chung also mentions the following "voices we might listen to":

my mother remembering Li Po's poem from her schooldays a 78 rpm record whose melody haunts me a Chinese Sarah Vaughn singing flowers . . . the Book of Songs . . . and the poets of Asian America George T. Chew Tomie Arai Fay Chiang Mei-mei Berssenbrugge Arthur Sze Jessica Hagedorn Alan Chong Lau Lawson Inada Garrett

Kaoru Hongo poems rooted in Chinese poetry . . . Jorge
Luis Borges Victor Hernandez Cruz.

Much of this literature came to Chung through dedicated
poetry publishers like New Directions and the Greenfield
Review Press or poet-led arts venues below 14th Street that
regularly held readings and workshops, such as Chinatown's
Basement Workshop and the Nuyorican Poets Cafe.
Chung emerged as a writer during a time of innovative cul-
tural and political syntheses in which community-based
groups looked to poetry in particular as archive, song,
protest, and spiritual cultivation.[9] Beginning with her first
publication in 1971, Chung's poetry exclusively appeared in
not-for-profit multicultural, women-of-color, or Lower
East Side journals and anthologies. She was not thereby
held to some rigid standard concerning the expression of
ethnicity, gender, or locale, as can be seen from the publica-
tion of her poem about the plight of a wifeless restaurant
worker in the *Asian Women's Journal* or *The Portable Lower
East Side*'s inclusion of a pantoum set in a Chinese village.[10]

D. Over Time

The ILGWU seems to consider Chinese women difficult to
organize, because they are thought to be passive and tied to
Chinatown's political and social structure. But in the sum-
mer of 1982, during the negotiation of a new contract, this
stereotype still shared by so many was shattered.

—PETER KWONG, *The New Chinatown*

Frances Chung's mother, Chee Kin Chung, joined in the
landmark demonstrations of 1982. She and her mother-in-
law, Hazel Quock, eventually worked in Chinatown cloth-
ing factories for a staggering total of seventy years. As is
common in the case of garment workers, unionization
helped procure health insurance, but failed to make employ-
ers honor minimum-wage laws. Defiant organizing and
protest over such issues as payment of back wages, childcare,

and unreimbursed overtime were part of the highly charged context in which Chung wrote.

In the "Crazy Melon" prose piece that begins "Lunchtime at the factory . . . ," Chung's depiction is both warm with the conversation of spirited women working together and coldly punctuated by the relentless clocktime of piecework:

> The loudspeaker plays Chinese music to make you think that you are in a Chinese movie, at home, or relaxing in Canton. Overtime is natural. And the talk. Are goldfish eyes hereditary then? Husbands. This one cooks dinner for me. My stupid one left me because I didn't give him children. What I make each day is not enough to buy a chicken.
>
> When the sewing is good (prices are high) at the factory, the women are happy. They say that they are eating 'soy sauce chicken.' One woman says that she takes the number 11 bus to work, meaning her two legs.
>
> The factory ladies, grateful for elevators and drafts of fresh air, develop a bent back from their positions at work. . . .
>
> The threads in your machine are entangled. You have made a mistake and must take apart your sewing. Beyond the fire escape you can see into other factories, through replicas of your own dust-ridden window. Lunchtime is suddenly over.

The perseverance of the women in Chung's extended family helped her imagine past heroes and rebels who emboldened her own efforts as a writer. A path to poetic predecessors was also provided through her parents' knowledge of Chinese literature; Chung would sometimes tape-record them reciting classical poetry at her request.

> born here yet breathing the air of another place
> with the blood of independent silkwomen in my veins
> different textures roll off my tongue
> no telling what I might say

E.

```
my Italian neighbor
spits down on the Chinese man
selling vegetables downstairs
Catholic school Italians push and bump
into old and young Chinese on Mott Street
```

From the unpublished poem "Abuse"

F. *"worms in books, clothes, or wood"*

The typical American encounters Chinatown as part of a process of alimentary gratification.

—JAN LIN, *Reconstructing Chinatown*

> see what you can behind the dragon lights
> the taut faces that mask thought and feeling
> (the bus leaves for the Statue of Liberty at two)
> Chinatown is a place to go eat chinks

Frank Chin calls it "food pornography": making a living by exploiting the "exotic" aspects of one's ethnic foodways. . . . Food pornographers seem to take pride in their apartness from the mainstream . . . to be acknowledging and proclaiming, not playing down, their difference. Nevertheless, what they in fact do is to wrench cultural practices out of their context and display them for gain to the curious gaze of "outsiders." . . . When the Chinese emigrate to America, the eating of "unusual" foods [carries the] dual connotation of brutalizing poverty and refined gourmandism. . . . The former connotation reinforces the white stereotype of Chinese as an outlandish, almost subhuman, race; the latter fits into the image of an overripe civilization that can teach the puritanical young nation a thing or two about sybaritic pleasures.

—SAU-LING CYNTHIA WONG, *Reading Asian American Literature*

> oh lucky me
> I am of some use
> I am of some inspiration
> to the two men

across the lunchcounter
I remind them of the
last Chinese restaurant
they took their family to

The commodity proliferates along the [arcade's] margins and en-
ters into fantastic combinations, like the tissue in tumors.—The
flâneur sabotages the traffic. Moreover, he is no buyer. He is
merchandise.

—WALTER BENJAMIN, *The Arcades Project*

Sau-ling Cynthia Wong's description of food pornogra-
phy ("what they in fact do is to wrench cultural practices out
of their context and display them for gain to the curious
gaze of 'outsiders.'"[11]) ironically dovetails with Benjamin's
exposition of allegory as a violent wresting of an image from
its mundane temporality: "To interrupt the course of the
world—that was Baudelaire's deepest intention."[12] Benja-
min goes on to say: "That which the allegorical intention
has fixed upon is sundered from the customary contexts of
life: it is at once shattered and preserved. Allegory holds fast
to the detritus."[13] The danger that allegorical detritus
might degrade into pornographic display always threatens
to corrupt Chung's treatment of "Chinese" objects or "Chi-
natown" scenes. It is instructive, therefore, to point out
ways in which her poetry thwarts such degradation.

Tourism is inseparable from the consumption of souve-
nirs, a consideration that provokes questions about Chung's
work since one of her techniques was to "collect" scenes and
language from disparate cultures and either set them loose
in streaming montages or rearrange them in emblematic se-
ries according to firmly imposed criteria, such as a color or
type of fruit.[14] But, as Benjamin insists, the collector is also
an allegorist whose "concern [is] the transfiguration of
things," and to whom

falls the Sisyphean task of divesting things of their com-
modity character by taking possession of them. . . . The

collector dreams his way not only into a distant or bygone world but also into a better one. . . . To dwell means to leave traces. In the interior, these are accentuated.[15]

One such interior would be that of modern lyric poetry, and Chung frequently conceived of literature as oneiric, as in "Pacific Avenue," "Celebration," and the untitled poems that begin "The cockroach dream nightmare . . ." and "Discovery of the secret power to / dream in Chinese." Chung's microscopically focused attention on a cockroach's footprint, the domesticity of a snail stolen from the Italian market, or "the tree along Canal Street that I / call my tree because it mirrors my / inner seasons" can be considered instances of what Benjamin characterized as interiorized "accentuation." The apparent contradiction between the two forms of breaking objects away from contexts—pornographic and allegorical—can be resolved by seeing the latter as the poet's re-collecting intervention in the former's deterritorializing rapaciousness. This provides a powerful rationale for Chung's miniaturizing poetics, its recrystallization within extremely brief and rigorous verse of not only the abject refuse of racism, tourism, cultural displacement, and urban poverty, but also of tableaux of intimate (or intimately felt) experience, often stabilized in frameworks that Chung constructed from her knowledge of literary and folk cultures. This is so despite the vast difference in circumstances between the bourgeois collector or flâneur and the young daughter of an immigrant working-class family stepping both inward (into a "secret book entitled Crazy Melon") and outward (into neighborhoods and readings) to make opulent poems from vermin, childhood memories of the street, and an overcrowded, brutally exploited district in which, nonetheless, she sees swirling mah-jong tiles and spent leaves in a teapot flower.

•

The effect in much of Chung's poetry is not prophetic (revelation of all to all), but the creation of deeper silences in which to safeguard personal or community thought, feeling, and relationships from the onslaught of real estate speculation, food pornography, exploitation by the garment industry, and the ideology of a nation at war against yet another Asian populace, the Vietnamese.[16] Thus, the poet, going her "separate ways on Sundays," may simply choose to turn her back on the trivializing curiosity of readers ignorant, for instance, of the legendary poet Li Po's "middle name."[17] (This is also one reason why the eroticism in Chung's poetry is so effective, eschewing the "self"-commodifying display of difference from a subjugated social position that Wong delineates in regard to food pornography.)

There is a risk, however, in viewing Chung's work as a sort of ethnic separatism. For to do so uncannily repeats the narrative often used to characterize Chinatown as a mysterious enclave that, due to its irreparably odd and foreign ways, removes itself from or "transcends" the social services and recourse to legal institutions of U.S. society in general. This narrative, of course, erases the history of racism and physical, judicial, and economic violence that originally pressured Chinese Americans to live together in separate communities.

There are several obvious responses one can make to this problematic. In many instances Chung directly lashes out at sexual and ethnic stereotyping and harassment, affectionately tells of the students in the ethnically diverse classes she taught, reverentially presents scenes from daily life that (as of yet) fall below the desire of touristic commodification, and sympathizes with neglected or ostracized neighbors barely surviving their drudgery, estrangement, or madness. She also relates gendered, economic features of Chinese diasporic history that are not easily made quaint or "ancient" in orientalist frameworks.

But, of course, the threat of appropriation comes from within Chinese and Chinese American constructions of identity as much as from mainstream ideology. Chung's intriguing redirection of such "internal" pressures is one reason why her work should be considered precocious and intrepid, fulfilling a role that is given little mention in sociological or political studies on Chinatowns. This is perhaps because the cultural production they do analyze is in the form of socially oppressive or (self-)mystifying official culture, such as the Taiwan Nationalist government's overseas promotion of pride in Chinese civilization or the Chinese-language media's appeal to supposedly commonly shared, timeless Confucian values to discourage "American-style" litigation, protest, or unionization by Chinatown's working class.[18] Such invocations, Peter Kwong asserts, are shared with state and business interests at-large to conceal actual economic conditions:

> the preference to live in Chinatown is hardly cultural. Chinatown, after all, has always been a ghetto plagued by poverty, crowded housing, unsanitary conditions, and crime, and deficient in American legal protection and the rule of law. Few Chinese would spend their lives there if they could help it, yet the American public continues to believe that Chinese are unwilling to assimilate into American society and to learn English. Over the years, this cultural self-segregation argument has grown into a fanciful theory.[19]

It is in this very context, however, that Chung's poetry proves especially agile in the way it cuts across Canal Street. Her depictions of *Chinatown*'s consumption of Chinese popular culture emphasize its phantasmatic status and delusive purpose, as in the "Crazy Melon" pieces that begin "The movie theater filled with sticky soda . . . ," "There is a group of Chinese-American men . . . ," and "Lunchtime at the factory . . ."—"The loudspeaker plays Chinese music to make you think that you are in a Chinese movie, at home, or relaxing in Canton. Overtime is natural." Chung does not annex Chinatown to China so much as reveal its continual production of imaginary relations with "China."[20] Moreover, her lateral movement across adjoining downtown cultures—

partly enabled by her "power to dream in four languages" ("Celebration")—worries the foundations of any vertical hierarchy of Chinese fidelity and order.

A wry illustration of this movement is the poem "Double Ten (10/10 day)," its title referring to the Republic in Taiwan's national day of celebration. Chung's Double Ten Day, rather than conform to coercive narratives of Chinese history, politics, or timeless identity, transmutes the three "Chinese" things that do appear in the poem by wresting them away from official nationalist time—its calendar of commemorations—through the heated intimacy of the speaker's love affair with an African American. In scenes that are anathema to Chinese ethnic communion, this lover is drawn to what is probably a jade pendant the speaker is wearing and sings a "Chinatown ballad" (while she sings a Billie Holiday song), and his erotic attraction is metaphorized as "the strong smell of black mushrooms." On the most heavily Kuomintang-supported holiday—during which Chinatown association heads can expect to receive emoluments from KMT representatives—the only sign of national community is an old Ukrainian neighborhood the lovers pass through while walking in the East Village.

G. *"a stroke to the right in writing"*

Maria Damon has noted that the "episodic" quality of "Crazy Melon" is "part of its beauty and significance."[21] Obviously, this has much to do with the perceptual dynamics of the urban scenes Chung describes—the sudden movement of things caught up in commerce, of quick switchings of focus from far to near, from out in the street to inside the family's small apartment. Secondly, it is reminiscent of the perceptual structures of certain outstanding Chinese lyric poems that Chung read, e.g. those of Wang Wei, in which sudden close-ups and reversals of visual frame are subtly made. It is also a result of the vast number of untold stories, unnarrated lives that Chung senses all around her. Chung developed a form of poetry that was particularly skilled at maneuvering the endless series of cultural and historical transpositions that Chinatown produces.

On the other hand, if we focus too much on her juxtaposition of ethnically marked objects and cultures, we miss the explicit compositional forms and figures she used, whether a pantoum, parataxis, or the following of an idea (tulips, chopsticks, a flower, three daughters) through a series of evenly phrased contexts. The poems are not collages or photographs, as if the poet were only a darting, naming eye: their tension and movement are generated by the linguistic implications she sets up, whether through allusion or phonetic, prosodic, and grammatical patterning. Although the rapid clarity of her seen images and the brevity of her poems associate by habit with the camera as a model, a more apt metaphor is the one with which she chose to end "Crazy Melon": the dictionary. In the final poem, which begins with the line "scenes gathered from a Chinese-English dictionary:," the poet revels in selecting phrases that are evocative precisely because they are untranslatable—crucial elements (of plot, context and connotation) are left unspecified in idioms like "clouds clearing away," "silence of three minutes," or "fireflies at the window and snow on the table." Fluency characterized Chung's movement *across* languages—English, Spanish, Cantonese dialect, the Chinese logograph—in which she possessed varying degrees of competence. Each shift instantly created depths and connections that could not be revealed from any one site, more so if one takes into account that they played differently across the minds of each listener or reader proficient in a different coordination of tongues.

In a poem like "of three minds," each line is formed by the pressure of what could not be stated or translated as much as by any quasi-geometric correspondence to scenes or events. The writing subject in Chung's poetry is never completely coterminous with a single national language, and in this it is like Cha's *DICTEE*, in which Naoki Sakai has discerned "the trace of an effort to sustain a certain ironical distance from the mother tongue. . . . For [Cha], every language is a foreign language." Sakai then asks, "But is it only for her that every language is a foreign language?"[22] *Crazy Melon and Chinese Apple* provides a deceptively clear answer to this question. Chung's New York Chinatown is home, but only if she has the freedom to claim it in perpetually brave and foreign terms that whisper routes to/from yet other neighborhoods where, as in "En busca del barrio chino de Lima . . . ," crazy etymologies of her middle name linger.

Notes

1. Jan Lin, *Reconstructing Chinatown* (Minneapolis: U. of Minnesota Press, 1998), p. 10.

2. Juliana Chang, "Reading Asian American Poetry," *MELUS* 21.1 (Spring 1996): 81–98, p. 93.

3. For treatments of Cha's *DICTEE* from an "interlingual" perspective, see, among others: Chang, "Reading Asian American Poetry"; Naoki Sakai, *Translation & Subjectivity* (Minneapolis: U. of Minnesota Press, 1997), pp. 18–39; Eun Kyung Min, "Reading the Figure of Dictation in Theresa Hak Kyung Cha's *DICTEE*," in Sandra K. Stanley, ed., *Other Sisterhoods: Literary Theory and U.S. Women of Color* (Urbana: U. of Illinois Press, 1998), pp. 309–24; Walter K. Lew, *Excerpts from: ΔIKTH DIKTE for DICTEE (1982)* (Seoul: Yeul Eum Sa, 1992), also online at <www.2.hawaii.edu/~spahr/dikte/>. For related issues in the larger context of Asian American poetry, see: WKL, "A New Decade of Singular Poetry," *Bridge: Asian American Perspectives* 8.4 (Winter 1983): 11–12; Brian Kim Stefans, "'Remote Parsee': An Alternative Grammar of Asian North American Poetry," in Edward Foster and Joseph Donahue, eds., *The World in Time and Space: Towards a History of Innovative American Poetry, 1970–2000* (Jersey City, N.J.: Talisman House, in press), pp. 130–64.

4. The statement is from Chung's New York State Council on the Arts Creative Artists Program Service fellowship application, May 30, 1980. Chung taught her trilingual poetry workshop in 1983 at the Poetry Project at St. Mark's Church in-the-Bowery.

5. The earliest dated poems that I have found in Chung's papers were written in 1967, when she was sixteen years old. Chung's work was completely neglected by a wide variety of such anthologies during the sixteen years between *American Born and Foreign, An Anthology of Asian American Poetry*, edited by Fay Chiang, Helen Wong Huie, Jason Hwang, Richard Oyama, and Susan L. Yung (Special double issue of *Sunbury: A Poetry Magazine* 7–8 [1979]), and my own *Premonitions* (New York:

Kaya Production, 1995). This was a matter of both lack of knowledge of the existence of her work and outright rejection of manuscripts she submitted.

6. Derived from the "seeing voice" in Michael Stephens, *The Dramaturgy of Style* (Carbondale: Southern Illinois U. Press, 1986).

7. All Nishiwaki quotations are taken from Hosea Hirata, *The Poetry and Poetics of Nishiwaki Junzaburō: Modernism in Translation* (Princeton: Princeton U. Press, 1993).

8. These titles are selected from a slightly longer list compiled by Frances Chung's older sister, Edna Chung.

9. For a vivid sense of the importance given to Asian American poetry at the time, see, among others, Dale Yu Nee, " 'See, Culture is Made, Not Born . . . ,' Asian American Writers Conference," *Bridge: An Asian American Perspective* 3.6 (August 1975): 42–48. For recollections of the Basement Workshop, see Fay Chiang, ed., *Basement Yearbook 1986* (New York: Basement Workshop, 1986), and Fay Chiang, "Looking Back: Basement Workshop, 1971–86," in Juliana Chang, ed., *Quiet Fire: A Historical Anthology of Asian American Poetry 1892–1970* (New York: Asian American Writers' Workshop, 1996), pp. 106–15.

10. Maria Damon makes a similar point about the simultaneously politicized and "historically, geographically, ethnically specific," yet "increasingly internally heterogenous . . . already-multiply signifying designator[s]" "NuYorican" and "Puerto Rican" in her "When the NuYoricans Came to Town: (Ex)Changing Poetics," *Xcp: Cross-Cultural Poetics* 1 (1997): 16–40, esp. 19–21. See also Miguel Algarín's and Bob Holman's opening essays in Miguel Algarín and Bob Holman, eds., *Aloud! Voices from the Nuyorican Poets Cafe* (New York: Henry Holt, 1994). Untitled poem ["he was growing old . . ."], *Asian Women's Journal* (1971; rpt. Asian American Studies Center, UCLA, 1976): 95; "Sa Gow," *The Portable Lower East Side* (1990): 124.

11. Sau-ling Cynthia Wong, *Reading Asian American Literature: From Necessity to Extravagance* (Princeton: Princeton U. Press, 1993), p. 68.

12. Walter Benjamin, *The Arcades Project*, trans. Howard Eiland and Kevin McLaughlin (Cambridge, MA: Harvard U. Press, 1999), p. 318.

13. Benjamin, *The Arcades*, p. 329.

14. Susan Stewart, *On Longing: Narratives of the Miniature, the Gigantic, the Souvenir, the Collection* (1984; Durham: Duke U. Press, 1993).

15. Walter Benjamin, "Paris, the Capital of the Nineteenth Century" <Exposé of 1935>, in Benjamin, *The Arcades*, p. 9. Theodor Adorno asserted that Benjamin's philosophy "appropriates the fetishism of commodities for itself: everything must metamorphoze into a thing in order to break the catastrophic spell of things." Quoted in Rolf Tiedemann, "Dialectics at a Standstill: Approaches to the *Passagen-Werk*," in Benjamin, *The Arcades*, p. 943.

16. See Chung's poem in "Chinese Apple" that begins "viet nam / bomb . . ." For a depiction of New York Chinatown's political, economic, and social situation around the time Chung began to write, see Rocky

Chin, "New York Chinatown Today: Community in Crisis," in *Roots: An Asian American Reader*, ed. Amy Tachiki, Eddie Wong, and Franklin Odo (Los Angeles: Asian American Studies Center, UCLA, 1971), pp. 282–95. Also, Peter Kwong, *The New Chinatown*, rev. ed. (New York: Hill and Wang, 1996), and Lin, *Reconstructing Chinatown*. For a rich analysis of phases of orientalism in New York prior to the Chinese Exclusion Act of 1882, see John Kuo Wei Tchen, *New York Before Chinatown, Orientalism and the Shaping of American Culture 1776–1882* (Baltimore: Johns Hopkins U. Press, 1999).

17. The two quotations are from, respectively, the "Crazy Melon" prose piece that begins "My Italian girlfriends dressed up . . ." and "For Li Po," the inital poem of "Chinese Apple."

18. Kwong, *The New Chinatown*, pp. 101, 139–40.

19. Ibid., pp. 202–3.

20. The question of which nation-state "China" actually refers to—the communist People's Republic of China or capitalist National Republic in Taiwan—was one that was hotly contested in Chung's community.

21. Maria Damon, personal communication, March 1999.

22. Sakai, *Translation & Subjectivity*, p. 31. Chung's relation to Chinatown shares much with Trinh T. Minh-ha's redefinition of diasporic identity as ways of re-departing from a "striated" origin in her essay "Cotton and Iron" (republished in Trinh T. Minh-ha, *When the Moon Waxes Red: Representation, Gender, and Cultural Politics* [New York: Routledge, 1991], pp. 14–15).

ACKNOWLEDGMENTS

Some of the poems in *Crazy Melon and Chinese Apple* were previously published in the anthologies *Ordinary Women: An Anthology of Poetry by New York City Women*, ed. Sara Miles, Patricia Jones, Sandra Maria Esteves, and Fay Chiang (1978); *American Born and Foreign: An Anthology of Asian American Poetry*, ed. Fay Chiang, Helen Wong Huie, Jason Hwang, Richard Oyama, and Susan L. Yung (1979); and *Premonitions*, ed. WKL (1995), as well as in a special literary issue of *Bridge: Asian American Perspectives*, ed. WKL and Shanlon Wu (1983), and the "Without Ceremony" issue of *IKON*, ed. Kimiko Hahn (1988). Several poems also appeared in *Yellow Pearl*, *The Asian Women's Journal*, *American Rag*, *The Portable Lower East Side*, *The Asian Pacific American Journal*, and *Chain*.

The editorial work for this book benefited from the care and contributions of many people. I express my appreciation to Frances Chung's entire family, but especially her older sister Edna Chung and her father Wilbert Chung for their constant faith, ideas, and supplying of materials. Juliana Chang assisted in the documentation of Frances Chung's papers and also gave insightful suggestions in regard to the supplementary essays, as did Maria Damon, Alvin Lu, David Schaberg, Brian Kim Stefans, and Suzanna Tamminen. I also thank Suzanna's colleagues at Wesleyan University Press, Thomas Radko and Matthew Byrnie, and at the University Press of New England for their wise and skillful shepherding of the book through the process of publication. Cover designer Charles Yuen provided keen advice on many aspects of book design and production. Aimee Kwon helped to proofread the originally submitted manuscript, and Ana Cheaz perused Chung's Spanish text. Gratitude is also owed to Eugene Ahn, Tomie Arai, Emily Bass, Fay Chiang, John B. Duncan, Heinz Insu Fenkl, Jewelle Gomez, Kimiko Hahn, Patricia Ikeda-Nash, Patricia Ann Spears Jones, Marjorie Lee and the student staff of UCLA's Asian American Studies Center Reading Room, Jinqi Ling, Won-Soon Park, Michael D. Shin, Quincey Troupe, Dorothy Wang, Shengqing Wu, and John Yau for their diverse assistance: "bravo for wondrous circumstance."

February 15, 2000   WKL
New York–Los Angeles